# THE NEW AVATAR

## AND

# The Destiny of the Soul

### THE FINDINGS OF NATURAL SCIENCE

### REDUCED TO PRACTICAL STUDIES IN PSYCHOLOGY

By

## JIRAH D. BUCK, M.D.

TO THE

# GREAT FRIENDS

THE HELPERS—VISIBLE AND INVISIBLE—

WHOSE DEEPEST MOTIVE AND HIGHEST AIM

ARE TO ENCOURAGE, UPLIFT, AND INSPIRE

## THOSE WHO NEED;

THAT ALL, AT LAST, MAY STAND

## TOGETHER

IN THE MIDST OF

THE

RADIANT SPLENDOR

OF

## ETERNAL

## TRUTH

# FOREWORD

The reader who is willing to give the following pages a careful reading, and a courteous hearing, is entitled to know the basis of study, observation or experience from which the suggestions, inferences and conclusions proceed, in order that he may fairly estimate their value.

At the age of seventy-two, my egotism is at least softened by the discovery of the many things I do not know; and my dogmatism, so far as it ever existed, is equally relaxed by the realization that it is a bar to light and knowledge, which rest so largely on demonstration.

For more than forty-five years I have been engaged in the active practice of medicine with consultations extending over three States.

For an equal length of time I have lectured in Medical Colleges, fifteen years on the subject of Physiology, an equal number on Therapeutics (including Pathology and Histology), and for the last fifteen years on Psychology, Mental and Nervous Diseases, and all this time with a large College Clinic from the poorer classes.

From first to last, my "Study of Medicine" has been generically and specifically a "Study of Man," physical, mental, ethical, and psychical.

Outside of Medicine as a "Calling" or a "Profession" my real interest has been to unravel the nature of man, grasp the problem of human life, and to apprehend the nature, laws, and destiny of the human soul. My library covers a rather continuous thread from , and the time of Paracelsus, to Profs. James, Ladd, Lombroso, Sir Oliver Lodge, and Münsterberg.

My reading dips into the Sacred Books of the East, the records of the Past, and particularly the psychic phenomena of different ages, finding at last the Constructive Theorem clearer than anywhere else in the "School of Natural Science," from the fact that it is demonstrably cognizant of all preceding work, and definitely conforms to the strict demands of Science—Physical, Mental, Ethical, Psychical and Spiritual, and proves to be the very thing for which I have searched for nearly half a century.

The foregoing statements are not made to force credulity nor to assume authority. They simply mean—This is how, and where, and how long, I have been searching, largely, also at the bedside of the sick, the deranged and the dying; from the first breath of the little one that comes—

"Out from the shore of the Great Unknown
Weeping and wailing and all alone,"

to the death-damp and the last sigh of the aged; in one case at nearly one hundred and four years.

Once I found an old lady of eighty, dying. The "death-damp" on her brow; the "death-rattle" in her throat; the chin dropped, and no pulse at the wrist. She had a wayward son who had been promised due notice of any change, and he had been sent for. Speaking distinctly in her ear *I called her back*; the motive being the grief of her son at not bidding each other good-bye. The response was immediate. The "rattle" in her throat ceased. The pulse promptly returned. The mouth closed. Then I said—"open your eyes," which she promptly did with a gentle smile. "You are not going to do it," I said. "No," she replied. The son soon came in and received his mother's caress and blessing. At the same hour on the following day, she passed peacefully to the beyond, dying of old age. Had it been a "crisis" in disease, she might have recovered.

As a psychic phenomenon I never saw anything just like it. Had I before doubted the existence of a "separable soul," it would have ended all doubt. From the magnetic border of the "Great Divide" *with a sufficient motive*, I literally "called her back."

The evidence of the concreteness, and wholeness and self-awareness of the Individual Intelligence, functioning in and through, and separable from the physical body, was complete. No other explanation or conclusion would fit or cover the case at all. Had I been clairvoyant and able to *see* the entity, it would have been another link in a chain whose sequence pointed all one way. But even here I was not without a witness.

In another case, an old lady was dying. A "Platform Lecturer" (Mediumistic) was present and described, incidentally, what she saw. She was a good, clean, ignorant woman and only "controlled" on the Platform.

She described a vapor emanating from the body, as the "death-damp" increased, and outer "awareness" failed. This vapor seemed to adhere together until it stood near the head, rounded and nearly reaching the ceiling. Then the "spirit form" passed out from the top of the head, was inclosed in the ball of "vapor," and together they "floated away."

I found that she had never heard of the "Auric-egg" nor read a page of the old Eastern philosophy, and yet she had accurately described, step by step, what the Masters for ages declare occurs at death.

Science is the careful observation, demonstration and record of Facts, their orderly grouping or classification, and the logical and sequential conclusions resulting therefrom.

It is not a matter of opinion and belief, nor dogma and denial, no matter how large, respectable, and sincere may be the army of the dogmatists.

Take these suggestions and conclusions—my friend—for what you think them worth, since now you know how far they have grown from experience and the love and search for the simple Truth.

The temptation to quote and annotate from many authors is very great, but the material is so abundant that one scarcely knows where to begin, where to end; and as the address is solely to the reader of "average intelligence," and argument is eliminated as far as possible, many quotations could do little more than confirm opinions, and would extend beyond the limits designed by the author, or the brief space and popular form more desirable for the average reader.

Repetitions in the text seemed unavoidable for the reason, that at every phase of the subject I have continually to regard the Individual, and that aggregate called Society; the inner conscious life of *one*, and the associate elements and conditions regarding the many, and from different viewpoints.

Man, the Individual, is like a "wheel within a wheel," the larger circle being Humanity as a whole.

Nor does the thought or concept stop here. There is the relation of the Individual Intelligence we call MAN to the Universal Intelligence we call GOD, which as related to Nature is "In All, Through All, Over All, and Above All."

Not an "Absentee God," but Illuminant within and without revealing itself in what we call Love and Law.

Here "in brief" I rest the case and proceed to the evidence.

# INTRODUCTION

In "A Study of Man, and the Way of Health," first published twenty-one years ago, as a general outline for my classes of Medical Students, to enable them to grasp the real problem of life, and to emphasize the Study of Man, as basic in the Study of Medicine, the following epitome was placed in the Preface.

"The cosmic form in which all things are created and in which all things exist is a Universal Duality.

Involution and Evolution express the two-fold process of the One Law of Development, corresponding to the two planes of being, the Subjective and the Objective.

Consciousness is the central Fact of Being.

Experience is the only method of knowing.

Therefore, to Know, is to Become.

The Modulus of Nature, that is, the Pattern, after which she everywhere builds, and the *Method* to which she continually conforms is an Ideal, or Archetypical Man.

The Perfect Man is the anthropomorphic God. A living, potential Christ in every human soul.

Two natures meet on the human plane, and focalize in man.

These are the Animal Ego and the Higher Self. The one, an inheritance from lower life. The other, an overshadowing from the next higher plane.

The Animal Principle is Selfishness. The Divine Principle is Altruism.

However defective in other respects human nature may be, all human endeavor must finally be measured by the principle of Altruism and must stand or fall by the measure in which it inspires and uplifts Humanity.

The highest tribunal is the criterion of Truth, and the test of truth is by its use and beneficence. 'BY THEIR WORK YE MAY KNOW THEM.'

Superstition is not Religion; Speculation is not Philosophy; Materialism is not Science; but true religion, true philosophy and true science are ever the handmaids of Truth, and will at last be found in perfect harmony."

After more than twenty years of continuous and careful study since the foregoing was written, I must still confirm and emphasize these basic propositions to-day.

The attempt is herein made to apply them more particularly to the study of Psychology. To add to what was then discerned and designated as "the Modulus of Nature," an exact and comprehensive Theorem of Psychology.

I am well aware how presumptuous this would in certain quarters be considered, if there were the least probability that "those in authority" would read these pages at all. The motive is involved in the modulus, and I am quite content to leave it there, while the "common people," it is hoped, may find herein, as I have found in the search for more light, encouragement, inspiration, and hope. And these may lead to Understanding.

It is the farthest possible from my thought or wish to ignore or belittle the labors of earnest students and writers on Psychology.

But there is a habit of conservatism in Physical Science to-day, that in spirit and effect differs very little from Dogma and Orthodoxy in Religion. It concerns methods rather than results. It is generally incredulous through fear of being over-credulous. It is bound by tradition, or the records of the past, and its dogmas are deductions from the consensus of *opinions*, rather than "decrees in councils" or "Infallible Popes."

Occasionally a Scientist, like Sir Oliver Lodge, seems to be utterly rid of both credulity and incredulity, and for these, Science really means— "the Facts of Nature, demonstrated, classified, and systematized."

But for the "Common People," the average intelligent student, for whom Science and the pursuit of Knowledge is not a Profession, but a desire to know, and to understand, in order to be able to use wisely and well, it is of far less importance to know what others think or believe, deny or affirm, on the subject of Psychology, than to *realize* what are the faculties, capacities, and powers of their own souls.

Knowledge for the sake of knowledge, like "Art for Art's sake," is one thing, Knowledge for *use* in daily life, and for illuminating its pathway and  revealing the purpose and destiny of man, is something different indeed.

This hunger of the individual soul for real knowledge is perhaps the most patent "Sign of the Times."

The average intelligent individual has broken away from the traditions of the past, and yet found nothing to take their place. One result is empty churches, and the race for wealth, display, position, and power. Increased idleness begets dissipation, Paresis and Insanity increase, while wasted opportunity both shortens and embitters life.

A very large number of intelligent men and women realizing all this, and repelled by the almost contemptuous conservatism of so-called Science, swing to the side of credulity, and are robbed and exploited by charlatans. They believe the Truth *ought* to be forthcoming, and their intuitions and demands, though oft leading to sore disappointment, deserve a better fate.

It is for these, and for these reasons, that these pages are written, and with no other hope of fame or reward.

The demand is everywhere for Knowledge of the soul. Facts there are in abundance, but how far these facts are *demonstrated*, so as to constitute a basis of exact science, and how to classify and systematize them, the average intelligence does not know.

The Psychical Scientist claims to know, and undoubtedly does know, but he busies himself almost exclusively in gathering and verifying *more facts*. When asked by the average intelligence, "What does it all mean?"—the answer is, "Ah! there's the rub. *Wait!* Some day we *may* know."

The simple fact is that the Scientist is bewildered, while the theologian and the dogmatist appeal to Faith without Knowledge, and invoke miracle as in all past times.

Spiritualism has had its day and left an immense body of facts, while Mediumship and the dark circle are more often repudiated by intelligent professed Spiritualists. Satisfied as to conscious existence after death as a *fact*, they have learned how generally unreliable are many messages from departed friends, owing to conditions beyond their control; while the effect of surrender to so-called "spirit-control" contributes to neither health nor a well-balanced mind or character.

Hypnotism maintains a precarious hold, simply through juggling with the words, "Suggestion" and "Hypnosis." The professional hypnotist, yielding as he must to the public fear and condemnation of Hypnotism, advocates *Just a little of it!* under the false title "Suggestion," for the good it is claimed to do in such cases as the drink and drug habit. As though a little further *weakening of the will*, would ultimately tend to restore and strengthen it!

One is reminded of the baby in "Pendennis." The Mother "hoped the Lord would forgive her, because it was such a little one!"

Even the leaders in the "Emmanuel Movement" have deceived themselves by this sophistry, and while they applaud the temporary results, they seem unaware that they are still further weakening self-control and real character, by dominating the Will.

It is thus that ignorance, confusion and unrest, like waves of ocean, ebb and flow in the great human tides.

Through impatience and discouragement alone, many give up the quest for knowledge as hopeless, and while too well-balanced to drift into dissipation, they suffer from *ennui* and become pessimistic.

Real knowledge will not come all at once, like a vision, or a complete revelation.

The first real Light that comes will be that of Faith, a term generally misunderstood and misused.

Faith is the complete antithesis of blind dogma and superstition. It is born within the soul, and never imposed by outward authority enforced by fear.

"Faith is the soul's *intuitive conviction* of that which both reason and conscience approve."

To give intellectual assent to belief in God is one thing; to be able to declare with light and warmth that uplifts and inspires, "*I know* that my Redeemer liveth" is another thing entirely.

The impatience above referred to would see the end from the beginning, and know all about the development and destiny of the soul before it has learned the first lesson that guides and determines both.

When, however, Science and Religion clasp hands, and the facts of nature guided by the light of Faith, build character and guide progress, there is revealed a Philosophy of Life that needs little revision. It is like the compass that points continually to the pole, and gives unqualified assurance as to the *direction* we are going.

So also every step in the past enables us to get our bearings and verify our course by checking backward.

Faith is no longer a blind dogma, but a compass in the box of experience, the wise mariner's guide in the voyage of life.

If neither Science, Religion nor Philosophy, nor all together can thus come to the service of man, can not do it *now*, after all the weary centuries since Plato and Aristotle, we may as well write *qui bono* on our banners and trail them in the dust!

Even the theologies of the day, recognizing the dilemma and the difficulties, still cling to the miraculous, and to make the best of a bad bargain, offer dogma in the place of demonstration, and contradictory and blind belief in place of the light of Faith.

While they count thousands as nominally in their communion, the intelligent among all these have many "mental reservations."

The intelligent thought of the world flows past and beyond them.

The "Soul's intuitive conviction" agreeing with "both reason and conscience" holds and guides them, in spite of the verbal "confession of faith."

The Divinity of Jesus, the Christ, can be fully explained under natural and divine law, without invoking miracle.

The result of such explanation is to dethrone him from the altars of dogma and superstition, and enthrone him on the altar of Love in the heart of Humanity.

This is long delayed, but cannot be defeated.

# STUDIES IN PSYCHOLOGY

# CHAPTER I

## CLASSIFICATION OF FACULTIES, CAPACITIES, AND POWERS

Starting with the *Modulus of Nature*—an Ideal or *Archetypal Man*, and coming down to practical things in daily life—

. Man *is* an *Individual Intelligence*. This is taken as an empirical *fact*, patent to every intelligent individual.

The source and nature of intelligence itself need not here concern us. We may call it an *ultimate* that all the philosophies of the world have signally failed to explain. It is something that grows, increases or decreases, expands, becomes confused, according to the conditions of bodily organ and function, heredity, environment, personal effort and the like; but so far as we know, it is the same thing, large or small, wise or foolish. It is still, measure for measure, Individual Intelligence.

. The term *Individual* means distinct, concrete, relatively separate. Man being an Individual Intelligence; God is the Universal Intelligence. Just as the organism of man is involved in, and evolved from Universal Nature; so the Intelligence of man is involved in, and evolved from Universal Intelligence.

The empirical fact of the intelligence of man presupposes a "sufficient reason" or source. Still we do not know what God and Nature and Intelligence are. We only know *how they manifest*. Our intelligence enables us to observe, reflect, reason, and in some measure apprehend the *method* and *manifestation*.

I am not seeking to build nor unfold a "Philosophy." "Yes," someone replies, "but a philosophy is implied or involved."

Very well, let *it* unfold *itself*.

**3**. The next empirical fact of prime importance is, The Individual Intelligence, not of man, but which *is* man, is *aware of itself*, i.e., "self-conscious." It is able to distinguish between the self and the non-self.

**4**. Again, as to *consciousness*, as with intelligence: We know that man has it and uses it, and what it *does* to some extent; but we do not know what it *is*, intrinsically, nor do we need to know any of these *ultimates*. The effort to explain them has never ended in anything but confusion. We shall herein name them, and then pass them.

**5**. We have now postulated a self-conscious, Individual Intelligence, as the real man. Next we find this Man can *do* things, or *refrain* from doing; act, or refrain from action. This is called Initiative, Volition, Will.

**6**. This power of action and of choice, inspired by intelligence, aware of the self, adapts actions to ends. This involves reason and judgment.

**7**. In the course of experience along the lines of action or restraint, and observing results in either case, the individual desiring or preferring certain results to others, acquires more or less self-control. He controls himself to secure desired results.

Here then, in brief outline, are the basis and the elements of our Psychology. They are drawn from common observation and experience, and are verified by the facts of daily life—generally complicated, confused, or lost sight of in treatises on psychology.

Two of these factors, viz.: Consciousness and Will, enter into all psychological phenomena such as Hypnotism and Mediumship, and into every form of mental alienation, insanity, obsession and the like.

Moreover, by building out of mental phenomena a distinct entity—largely independent of the self-conscious Intelligence, and almost equally so with consciousness—our "philosophies," "metaphysics," and explanations have become as confused and unreliable as the psychical phenomenon itself.

Hudson's so-called "Law of Psychic Phenomena," "Subliminal" and "Supraliminal Consciousness," and the juggling with the terms "suggestion" and "hypnosis" may serve as sufficient illustrations. In each instance phenomena are made to take the place of principles and the core of the problem is ignored, confused, or lost sight of.

In the meantime these empiricists are hunting in the "rubbish of the temple" (which temple they have *metaphysically* destroyed), for the Human Soul—i.e. the concrete, intrinsic Individual Intelligence, which is ONE, and which the Master Builder (Universal Intelligence) placed on the Trestle-board of Creation and Time, for the building of character, and the evolution of the Human Soul.

If the Ideal, Archetypal, or Divine Man, is recognized as the *Modulus* of both Nature and Divinity, our Theorem must consist in adhering to the Modulus and working out the problem.

Q. E. D., if applied to man's completion of his own individual Temple, might stand for the last words of Jesus, "It is finished," The problem is solved; "I have finished the Work Thou gavest me to do." Science, Religion and Philosophy have clasped hands. Divinity revealed in Humanity is triumphant over Death. "There is a Natural (physical) body and there is a Spiritual body," and the Individual Intelligence is ONE in each, or in both; viz.: The Human-Divine Soul.

To recognize the *Modulus* and intelligently to apprehend the *Theorem* is the foundation and the first step in the scientific solution of the problem of life, and the progressive and continuous evolution of the human soul. To use the term "Science" (as applied to the study of psychology) in any other way, is pure empiricism, is wholly unscientific, and has never yet resulted in anything but confusion and in laying a foundation for belief, conjecture, theory, dogma, superstition, and fear.

The step of next importance, both in the scientific study of psychology and in individual progress and evolution, is the mental attitude of the individual; his point of view; his open-mindedness and utter refusal to *pre*judge anything. He will often say, "I do not know." He will sometimes say, "I do not care." That phase or presentation does not appeal to, nor interest him.

This is what the Vedic philosophers called, "making the mind *one pointed*" and like a search-light, with the ability to concentrate it on a given point or subject.

Bias, prejudice, preconceived opinion, credulity and incredulity, are all like a crooked lens to the eye of the mind, or to the perception of the simple truth.

Not only are these principles basic in the scientific study of psychology and the evolution of the individual intelligence, but their neglect and oversight are solely responsible for the confusion everywhere manifest on the subject, as well as for *every form of subjective control*, mediumship, psychical epidemics, and obsession, and they enter into every form and phase of insanity.

If this be true, and it is readily demonstrable, what subject is of equal importance; and what facts and considerations are so transcendent as these?

The difference is that between a mad-house with its frenzied and frightened mob of helpless victims, and a palace of the gods in which dwelleth Righteousness, Love, Peace, and Eternal Joy.

Is it not *worth while*?

This Modulus and Theorem of the School of Natural Science involve Religion, Regeneration, Redemption, and the well-being of Souls here and hereafter.

They separate Religion from Superstition, Duty from Dogma, cast out Fear, release the wings of aspiration and faith; and where "the mourners went about the streets" is heard a new song of rejoicing that binds up the wounds and sorrows of the brokenhearted.

Again I ask, "Is it not worth while?"

# CHAPTER II

## EMPIRICAL AND SCIENTIFIC EVIDENCE

Let us bear in mind that man *is* an Individual Intelligence; that this involves self-consciousness, or awareness of Self, the innate ability to distinguish between the Self and the non-Self. Hence arises the power of choice, discernment, or discrimination.

There also arises the impulse to *act*, or the Initiative, called the Will. This also involves the power of restraint, the act or the refraining from action.

This action, under the basic endowment—intelligence—is called *Rational Volition.*

There is thus, Intelligence; the Power to choose; the power to act and the adaptation of acts or restraints to ends, or to desired objects or results.

Experience teaches the individual, thus endowed, that he is responsible for all he thinks, feels, acts and does; and this, under his endowment of Intelligence, is what we call *Conscience.*

We are not building up a theory, but simply analyzing psychological facts, demonstrated as true in the experience of every intelligent individual. Just as the chemist analyzes a compound he finds in his laboratory.

Our *Modulus* is the Perfect Man. Our *Theorem* is the method of use that, by experience and observation everywhere, has been demonstrated as Constructive, enabling the Individual to build toward, and to realize the Modulus.

The power to discriminate, choose and act, when normally exercised, implies judgment and understanding.

Hence, we have perception, rational choice, intelligent action and desired results, for which we recognize our personal responsibility. Hence arise our ability and necessity to *review* our actions, motives, aims and their results, and to pass judgment upon them in the Light of Conscience (Con-Science, to know the Self) to pass judgment upon ourselves as to motives, aims, results, and consequences.

The Brain is a center of consciousness with avenues of perception and impulse and departments that by aggregation, separation or association, enable the Individual Intelligence to determine the relation in time, or duration, force and orderly relation of perceptions, desires, motives, actions (or thoughts and feelings) as to sequence or results.

This whole conscious realm is the Mind. It is the *inner chamber* of the *Soul*. It is in no sense an entity. The actor, the real entity, is the Individual Intelligence.

To say, therefore, that "Man is all mind," or that the mind does this, or that, is simply nonsense. It is like saying that the little room in which I am now writing, with its books and pictures, with my thoughts, feelings, emotions, and magnetism, is *I*! Perhaps it is *like* me, or *full* of me, but *I* am something *else* and something *more*.

Let us get rid of this "confusion of tongues"; this "babel of Psychology"; "New Thought" (as old as man);

"Metaphysics"; "Christian Science" *et hoc genus omne*, and come down to common sense and the facts of nature. The aim and the results along these lines are often good and helpful; then why clothe them in the garb of absurdities?

Recognize the facts, and express them intelligently, and they may do ten times more good, for then we could understand them. They are, one and all, a weak dilution of the old Hindoo Yoga, thrashed over there for thousands of years; straining after *results*, while ignorant of, or ignoring *basic principles*.

Aside from the "Eight Systems of Philosophy" now recognized in India, there are hundreds of varieties and classes of *Yogis*.

"To acquire powers" is one thing; self-mastery and self-knowledge are quite another. Thus the one is often distorted and always transient; the other constructive, regenerative, and enduring.

To illustrate by contrast what Constructive Psychology, or the building of character, *is not*, we may now take some of the forms of diseased action known to all time, occurring in individuals and in epidemics, and which to-day fill our Insane Asylums with "Incurables."

The point of first importance in all these cases, is the *lack* of self-control. Weakness, aberration or disease of the Will. The Individual Intelligence fails to exercise its divine prerogative and be *Master* in and of its *own house*.

In the place of this control, sensations, feelings, emotions, desires, appetites, passions, and ambitions run riot. The *Servants* of the Master war among themselves, quarrel with each other, bind the Master hand and foot, wreck the furniture, and at last destroy the house. The Master has become the victim and at last the slave of his own servants. His Will is in abeyance; his perceptions distorted; his feelings and emotions aggravated; his "Reason Dethroned"; his judgment impaired; he has an "Unbalanced Mind."

What is here needed but *Christos* in the Temple, "turning over the tables of the money-changers and the seats of them that sold doves," and restoring the High-Priest in the Holy Temple—the Human Soul, viz.: the intelligent Will of Man, determined to govern his own house, and responsible for results?

In place of Rational Volition, clear, just and true perceptions, sound judgment and clear understanding, we have "Illusions," "Hallucinations" and "Delusions." In other words, the Individual is *Insane*!

It all goes deeper than the *Mind*; the Soul, the Individual Intelligence is dethroned in his own Kingdom; Body, Mind, and Soul are out of joint.

Not only does this condition exist without being recognized; not only just here lies the whole secret and field of *Education* in child, woman and man, but so ignorant are thousands as to these patent facts and basic principles, that they covet and strive after this confusion, this devolution, in the vain search for knowledge, light, and truth.

These are the office, the function and the result to the subject (or victim) of Mediumship and Hypnotism. They yield the Will, the mastery of their own house, to another.

The servants may be tractable for a while, but an *alien* is seated upon the throne, and the Master is no longer King in his own realm.

Others may indeed learn something from his undoing, from the crimes committed upon him, just as we learn from criminals how we *ought not* to live.

Whether ignorantly, voluntarily, by persuasion, or by force of a stronger will, the medium and the hypnotic subject are victims either of ignorance or of design, to their own undoing.

These psychical experiences have been found in all ages and among every people of whom we have any valid history, from the red Indians of the North to the Voodoos of Africa, and from the Hill Tribes of India to the earliest Scandinavian Tribes and the islands of the sea.

As civilizations advanced, the more intelligent and unscrupulous individuals, ambitious of knowledge or power, regardless of the rights or well-being of others, and discovering these powers, exercised them for their own aggrandizement. This has been known through the ages as *Black Magic*, and is laughed at to-day by so-called "Scientists" as "nothing but the fears, credulity, and superstitions of the ignorant multitude." This was the core of Egyptian Paganism, and is the very genius of Clericalism to-day—the domination of the Individual Will, through superstition and fear.

Owing to seismic and cataclysmic shocks, volcanic eruptions, tidal waves, and great epidemics of disease, whole peoples have been dominated by fear or frenzied by superstitious dread, so that whole villages and cities became literally "mad-houses," and were often depopulated.

Read the story of "Peter, the Hermit," and "The Crusades," the "Black Death," the "Great Plague" that swept over Europe in the Thirteenth century; or that of the "Flagellants," and the "Dancing Mania," where whole villages became "Dancing Dervishes," samples of which may occasionally be found to-day in the cities of America, the "Yogis" that are "Buddhas" or "Christs" in New York, and the Dowies that were "Elijahs" in Chicago, the Genius of Point Loma, Obispo, Santa Rosa, "Oahspe," "Solar-Biology," and again, *et hoc genus omne*! Verily! "there is nothing new under the sun."

Contrast these individuals with an individual of sound mind, good judgment, and a well-ordered life, and see how and where and why the wreck inevitably follows.

The pressure outside changes continually, and these things spread and grow like all contagions. Nature at times seems wrathful and destructive, and there are, no doubt, deep-seated conditions and changes in the magnetism of the earth and air, not yet comprehended by modern science.

In stamping out contagious and epidemic disease, simple cleanliness has been like a revelation from the gods, and modern surgery has only stopped short of the miraculous.

Society is but the aggregation of individuals, and on the one principle of *Self-Control* every individual is related to the negative or the positive side of psychical and physical epidemics.

There is scarcely an avenue along these lines that has not been more or less explored by modern science.

That knowledge is still incomplete; that mistakes have been made; that matters have been contemptuously set aside, belittled, or declared to be not worth investigation, was to have been expected. But the progress has been immense, and the light shines on many obscure and difficult problems, where before was the utter darkness of superstition and fear, dirt, degradation, and death.

These phenomena manifest on the physical plane, disturb the social state, and the relations of individuals to each other. They concern the environment of man in a world of matter, sense, and time.

But the Individual Intelligence, which is Man, lives also in another world, related to, but within, around, and beyond the physical.

Man senses or feels it as anterior to birth and extending beyond death. He calls it the subjective or Spiritual World.

The realm of his consciousness is related to it, as the body is related to the physical plane and the things of sense and time. His consciousness seems *aware* of both planes or both worlds, though ignorant of the real nature and meaning of both, and capable of interpreting neither correctly.

Man feels his way through the life on the outer plane guided by his experience of weight, measure, distance, resistance, and the like.

The other world—the inner, or subjective—seems distant, evasive, and unreal, and in contemplating it he is filled with uncertainty, dread, fear, and superstition.

Our friends die and disappear; we miss them, and mourn for them. Where are they? What will become of us when we die? Shall we ever meet them again?

Passing by religion and revelation, as we are dealing with facts and phenomena in the natural life of man, rather than with creeds and dogmas that undertake to cut the "Gordian Knot," these questions stare everyone in the face, and in every age man has tried to solve them by actual knowledge.

Belief in ghosts, angels and demons is practically universal; and just here comes in the whole range of psychical phenomena, facts and fantasies, illusions, hallucinations and delusions, rational volition, reason dethroned, and the Will in Subjection, already referred to.

As individual experiences, subjective or objective, all are real. The fear incited by illusions and hallucination, or by "seeing a ghost," regardless of the fact of its actual existence, is as real to the individual as that of meeting a serpent in the grass, or a tiger in the jungle.

Soothsayers, diviners, prophets, mediums, conjurers, and seers consequently have been found in every age and among every people. Ignorance, fear, dread of death, desire to know, have always provided them with patrons, followers, or disciples.

They have often reaped a rich harvest, and not unfrequently dominated a race or a people, as the Papacy does to-day.

Where they have failed to create belief, they have often triumphed through fear and anathema, and often supplemented these weapons by persecution, imprisonment, torture, and death, and so held sway.

Revelation begs the question; dogma forces the conclusion; and both dominate the soul without convincing and without *knowledge*.

# CHAPTER III

## MEDIUMSHIP, SEERSHIP, AND HYPNOSIS

Into this arena of the inquiring soul of man, came Modern Spiritualism.

It contained little or nothing new, as to methods, aims, or results.

The Church, Protestant and Catholic alike, uttered their warnings, called it "dealings with the devil," but divested of political authority and without power to arrest or persecute, as in the past, were unable to stay the tide. It swept the country like a whirlwind. The average individual, desiring to know and to get tidings from departed friends, was unrestrained and unterrified.

He could not see why, if the gates were really ajar, angels might not communicate, no less than devils.

Then came the cry of "fraud," often amply justified, and a cloud of uncertainty and unreliability settled over the phenomena generally. Unscrupulous men and women seeing their opportunity, sophisticated and exploited it, and "exposures" of these became common.

But in spite of all this, there remained facts, and groups of phenomena impossible to explain away.

Finally, men like Crookes and Wallace took up the subject and investigated the phenomena, not from the emotional, expectant, or fraternal aspect, but from the purely scientific, and rendered their verdict, which, though frequently ignored or treated with contempt, remains practically unaltered.

Thousands became convinced of the *fact* of life beyond the grave, and at the same time of the unreliability of many so-called "communications." Finally the "Society for Psychical Research" was formed; phenomena were searchingly examined, verified, and recorded as a basis for further research.

The posthumous work of F. W. H. Myers, "Human Personality and its Survival of Bodily Death," added to the Society's records and many other publications a record of verified facts in psychic phenomena such as never before existed, and which nothing short of a cataclysm can destroy.

In the meantime, the "dark circle" went into desuetude, and Spiritualism, as a cult, declined. Accepting the broad conclusion of a life after death, and with no very clear demonstration as to exactly where, or how, the case rested largely.

The reason for this obscurity was to be found in the absence of clear conceptions as to the nature of the human soul, and what life on the spiritual plane really signifies.

In other words, the foundation was laid empirically to await classification and conclusions in a comprehensive Philosophy of Psychology, consistent with a science of the soul; and there it remains  to-day with the average individual, and the average man of physical or psychical science.

Returning now from this brief excursion into the social status, to the problem as related to the mental, moral, and physical health of individuals, and bearing in mind our Modulus of Man, and Theorem of Constructive Psychology, we find the annals of Spiritualism, Mediumship, or subjective control, of exceeding importance.

Another plane of life exists. Individuals on either plane communicate with the controlling entity on the supra-physical plane.

The Medium is invariably subjective and controlled. He has no choice of controls, and often no knowledge (never reliable knowledge) as to who or what controls him. He is sometimes informed by his "guide" as to the control's identity, and learns, often, that he and his circle have been deceived by ignorant or "lying spirits."

The whole process reverses our Modulus and Theorem of Constructive Psychology, the building of character and normal evolution.

The most important consideration at this point is its relation to the sanity of individuals.

There are thousands of individuals to-day, who, failing in rational volition, or self-control, are controlled by entities on the subjective plane. They are *obsessed*.

This subjective control without the knowledge or consent of the victim, and unrecognized and generally called "absurd" by "Alienists" and "experts," constitutes a very large per cent, of the insane to-day, and because ignored or unrecognized, these cases are classed as "Incurable."

It should be remembered that the annals of Spiritualism, and the records of scientific Psychical Research, have *demonstrated* the possibility and the *fact* of such control. It should also be remembered that the average "expert alienist" is guided solely by results of such obsession, where it occurs; that he is blind to causes, liable to exclude or taboo obsession, and therefore largely liable to err.

In other words, he is prejudiced; and his bias and incredulity blind him to the facts and to the real causes.

He could hardly be expected to make the obsession *let go*, while denying that it exists. But he *might* help the victim gain *Self-control* if he but recognized the facts and knew how.

Realizing the fact of the connection of the two worlds, the physical and the spiritual, and communication between them in the subjective or irresponsible way, the question naturally arises, "Is there not another way of communication? May not the Individual Intelligence on the physical plane communicate with the denizens of the spiritual plane *at his own volition, independently*? May he not learn to see and hear them without attempting, or desiring to *control* them, more than he does his associates, his friends and neighbors on the physical plane, or allowing them to control him?"

Is it not purely a question of *fact*, and of scientific demonstration, to be determined by experiment?

This question leads us to another phase of psychology and the records of the past. There have been Seers, Clairvoyants, and Clairaudiants in all ages.

Unlike the psychical phenomena already referred to,—and belonging to the positive and initiative, rather than the negative and subjective side of the psychical equation,—

these seers have been fewer in number, and are always individuals showing a high degree of self-control, and of intellectual and moral evolution.

Admitting the general propositions involved, it can readily be seen that this must be so from the very nature of the case. The Masters of mankind, in any and all directions have been few. The slaves, through ignorance, superstition and fear, have been legions. Those who have gained habitual self-control, and finally self-mastery, knowledge and power, have been few; while the majority have been controlled by their own appetites and passions, and by other individuals.

This self-mastery and higher evolution also includes another element beside strength of character, and that is, Refinement.

In other words; it is, from first to last, a journey from the gross and sensuous physical plane, toward the refined and spiritual plane, involving all the faculties, capacities, and powers, feelings, sensations, emotions, intuitions, and aspirations of man. It is, in short, a normal, higher evolution.

All the elements of this higher evolution arc basic and innate in the original endowment of man. By exercise, the latent faculties, capacities and powers grow, expand, and develop. Self-control, rational volition, and the sense of personal responsibility, (conscience) make the evolution conformatory to the Modulus—the Perfect Man.

As this human being, dwelling on the physical plane, *e*volves, the spiritual faculties of the Divine Man are *in*volved from the spiritual plane. When this simultaneous and co-ordinate development is complete, the Human and the Divine are *at-one* in the Individual.

This at-one-ment is the exact opposite of "vicarious." It is the result of personal effort and self-mastery.

The dogma of the church has so completely sophisticated it as to turn normal evolution into *devolution*; and, so far as it has any effect, or is operative at all, to turn man backward toward the animal, instead of upward toward the Divine.

Seership and Spiritual powers, therefore, as the result of "Living the Life," are *Evolutionary*. Mediumship, subjective control, and obsession in any form, or in whatsoever degree, are *Devolutionary*.

Progress along either line may be very slow, but the trend is as opposite as is the East from the West, as Light from Darkness, as Good from Evil.

By classifying these powers of man and psychical phenomena to which they give rise, whether in the conscious, inner realm, in functions of the bodily organism, or observable to others, we are able to assign each to its proper class with considerable accuracy.

Both evolutionary and devolutionary progress, with the ordinary individual, are slow processes. Seldom is either process a designed and straightforward climbing, or a quick descent "into the dark abyss."

Consequently, as the human race evolves as a whole, relatively more and more individuals are found who "get flashes" of sight or sound, more or less from the subjective or spiritual plane of being. There are intuitions, "warnings," and premonitions of coming events. Some seek and cultivate, others fear and avoid them.

They are mostly on the "border-land," if not on the "ragged-edge" of insanity. It is only necessary to further weaken the will, or to indulge the passions and emotions, in order to decide the matter, derange the mind, and send the individual to an asylum.

On the other hand, with individuals who lead a clean, cheerful, well-ordered life, these experiences may mean encouragement, confirmation, and progress toward the spiritual realm of being. They should be observed carefully, but not *cultivated*. They may serve as guide-posts and as mere incidents of a day's journey.

The average popular cult to-day, as often in the past, where psychical phenomena are involved, results  in converting the normal mental realm, the realm of normal self-consciousness, into a vaudeville performance; a mere "Variety Show," where all due sense of proportion and relation is lost.

In place of the normal Individual Intelligence, sitting serenely on the throne of life and ruling his Kingdom with justice, wisdom and paternal love, the king joins the melee of acrobats and dancing girls, encourages the orchestra till, in a pandemonium of revelry, he puts out the lights, or in wild frenzy fires the building.

Sometimes it claims to "command success" by *demanding* it; or wealth without earning it; or health without regard to hygienic law; or by "taking a Mantram" to open the gates of heaven. Or again, by servile obedience to the freaks or dogmas of a "Leader" or "Official Head" and adulation *ad nauseam*, to gain admission to the "Elect."

One and all of these, from first to last, tend toward Devolution. They are destructive, not constructive, in building character and true manhood and womanhood.

Again, the Monk or the devotee abandons society, becomes a recluse, flees into the desert or the mountain, subsists upon roots or herbs, sits in one posture till the joints of the body become fixed, holds the arms above the head till they become immovable, and the finger nails *turn and grow through the palms of the hands*; or sits gazing at the navel and repeating the word *Om*.

Indeed, it would seem that the ways and means to stop normal growth, constructive evolution and healthy living, had been well-nigh exhausted.

The enthusiast, the fanatic and the "easy mark" of to-day are seldom aware of any of these things, and so they are bled, fleeced, and exploited accordingly. "All is Mind!" "Great is Elijah!" or "Mrs." Elijah, and Oahspe is his Prophet! while Babel reigns in the place of Natural Science.

The Theosophical Movement inaugurated in this country by H. P. Blavatsky in , differed essentially and radically from all others; first, in placing ethics as the first stone in the foundation of a real knowledge of the nature of man. Its objects as concisely stated at the time were—

First: To establish a *nucleus* for a Universal Brotherhood of Man.

Second: To study ancient religions, philosophies and sciences, and determine their relations and values.

Third: To investigate the Psychical Powers latent in Man.

Hospitality to Truth from any source and under any name, was characteristic of the movement during the entire lifetime of the Founders.

Dogma was eliminated, Authority beyond facts and demonstrated truth denied, and Superstition regarded as only another name for ignorance.

While the facts and the demonstrations of Science were recognized, and given the largest hospitality, nevertheless, the "Secret Doctrine" and, in a broad sense, the whole movement was an effort to present to modern times, and particularly to the Western world, the most ancient and pure philosophy of old India, the *Vedanta* or "Wisdom-Religion."

An immense work of rejuvenation has gone on in India, particularly in the establishment and maintenance of Schools for Girls, and in the relief of poverty and discouragement of the teeming millions.

An immense literature was created, not yet appreciated, except by students here and there, who found light, explanation, and encouragement in their studies of the mysteries of Nature and of life.

Since the death of the founders of the Society, in this country at least, only a few branches and fragments of the original organization now remain.

"Leaders" and "Official Heads" often wholly ignorant of the Philosophy, which colossal egotism and exploitation could hardly supply, have brought the very names "Theosophy" and "Brotherhood" into contempt and ridicule in many sections.

As some of these "official heads" are still in evidence, final results cannot now be formulated, and need not be here considered or forecast. The evidence is not all in.

Personally, I desire to record my great indebtedness and highest appreciation of a noble life and a magnificent work accomplished by one of the most remarkable and unselfish women known to history, and for the light and knowledge which she made accessible, and which I still hold, practically unchanged,  but with the theorems of Natural Science, in place of the postulates of Philosophy as better fitting "the progressive intelligence" of the present time.

The two lines of presentation when clearly apprehended are not antagonistic, but supplementary. Their aims and purpose are the same.

# CHAPTER IV

## THE MEASURE OF VALUES

This is a very utilitarian age. Start almost any subject, propose almost any scheme, adventure, or investment, and the question is asked, "Will it pay?" The multitude are cautious; the lower stratum, the unsuccessful—the poor and the oppressed—are envious and often bitter and resentful; the successful are often reckless, dissipated, and proud.

I am not writing an essay on Economics, but on Ethics and Psychology; on the character, value, and use of the resources *within* ourselves; our *real possessions*. Here only may be found *actual values*.

I am not considering the "hereafter," as to "rewards and punishments"; what gods, devils, angels, or men may do *to us*, here or hereafter; but what we may (if we choose) do *for ourselves*.

This question is practical to the last degree. Put the question, "does it pay?" and I answer: It pays like nothing else on earth; it is the only thing that is independent of time, place, or circumstance.

It concerns man's *actual possessions*, of which nothing in "the three worlds" can ever dispossess him. I know of nothing so beneficent, in any concept of God or Nature, Providence or Destiny, as this birthright and opportunity of man, to build character, and *be* what he chooses to be.

He who knows his power, realizes his opportunity and utilizes his resources, may build a Palace of the Soul, in which he may dwell, literally, in a "kingdom of heaven."

And because God is the Architect, and Man the Contractor and Builder, working strictly to the "plans" and the designs, "that house shall stand." It is founded on the "Rock of Ages."

Did anyone ever know or see a noble character that was not built by the Individual himself, by personal effort, by self-control, by self-denial, by justice and kindness to others; often in the face of Poverty; often in spite of wealth; often in the face of sickness, pain and deformity; perhaps deaf and dumb and blind; and yet, like Helen Keller, the soul triumphant and glorified?

To-day, as I write, I went to the Crematory to see the dissolution of a poor, twisted, deformed, and tortured body of a woman past fifty, in which had dwelt a soul so serene, cheerful, and patient, that the beatitudes clustered around her, like doves in a garden of roses. It required no stretch of the imagination to determine what society she had entered. "Like seeks like," and each "goes to his own place." Her motive, the day-star of her life, was the Mother-Love for an only son. In spite of poverty and pain, she must reward him for love and loyalty, by being bright and cheerful and by belittling her own discomfort to save him sorrow.

Her reward was the growth of the soul that has now risen to its great reward, and dearer and sweeter than all this to the Mother-heart, was to see and realize the growth, the tenderness, and the beautifying of the soul of the Son.

Did it pay? I can almost hear her shouting for joy as she joins the anthem of the Invisible Choir of Helpers that welcome her just over the border. She prayed many times, even the last time I saw her, before the great change, "If it be possible, let this cup pass from me." I could only say, "Wait just a little longer," with the assurance that every shadow of darkness shall be transformed into dazzling light, and every drop of bitterness into the nectar of the Gods. She was almost deaf and blind, but you should have heard the sweetness in her voice and seen the radiance in her face. I did not know that the end was so near.

To the son, the sweetest sound on earth was that mother's voice, but, though silent for a thousand years, he would not recall her to one moment of the old torture. His sorrow for *himself* is swallowed up and glorified in his joy for her release.

And what is all this but a lesson in practical psychology, the growth of the soul?

Does it pay? Ask that Mother; ask that Son now. "How do you know?" How do you know anything, except as you see, or experience it?

Character reveals itself. It cannot long hide itself.  When the check goes to the bank the resources are there. The Bank of God, and of Nature, and of Compensation, and Eternal Justice, cannot fail. Its resources are infinite.

Independent of time, place, or circumstance, I said: Intrinsic, Inalienable.

Take another illustration almost at random. A cultured soul, winning its way alone, and at great disadvantage.

In the middle of the tenth century lived Farabi, or Alfarabi. He did not confine himself to the Koran, but fathomed the most useful and interesting sciences. He visited Sifah Doulet, the Sultan of Syria. The Sultan was surrounded by the learned who were conversing with him on the sciences.

Farabi entered the salon where they were assembled and remained standing till the Emperor desired that he should be seated; at which the philosopher, by a freedom rather astonishing, went and sat on the end of the Sultan's sofa. The Prince, surprised at his boldness, called one of his officers and commanded him, in a tongue not generally known, to put out the intruder. The philosopher heard him, and replied in the same tongue, "O Signor! he who acts so hastily is subject to repent." The Prince was no less astonished by his reply than by his manner and assurance.

Wishing to know more of him, he began a conference among his philosophers, in which Farabi disputed with so much eloquence and energy that he reduced all the doctors to silence. Then the Sultan ordered music, and when the musicians entered, Farabi accompanied them upon the lute with so much delicacy as to win the admiration of all present. He then drew out, at the Sultan's request, a piece of his own composition, and sang it with his own accompaniment, and had the audience first in laughter, and then in tears—and to complete his Magic, changed to another piece and put them all asleep.

The Sultan in vain urged Farabi to remain near his person, and offered him a high position in his household.

Voluminous writings of Farabi are preserved in the library at Leyden.

"A tale of the Arabian Nights," you may say, and yet it is historic. It reveals the fact that resources, character, and wisdom, in the end triumph and surmount all obstacles. They are intrinsic and permanent values.

They may remain unknown or unappreciated by others, but they are none the less riches to him who possesses them.

It was during this same tenth century in which Alfarabi lived, that there existed at Baghdad a Society composed of Mohammedans, Jews, Christians, and Atheists, for the purpose of Philosophical discussions and scientific investigation; and it was doubtless under this influence that Alfarabi was educated and enabled to cope with the philosophers of the world. Here in Arabia was the highest culture known at the time, in Medicine and all the Arts and Sciences, while the Ecclesiastics were inaugurating the dark ages elsewhere, to eventually spread over the whole of Europe.

Here and there have always appeared individuals superior to their age and time; men who dug to the foundations of knowledge, built character, accumulated resources, and left their impress upon all subsequent time.

Nor has this accumulation of real knowledge been derived from books and schools, though these resources have not been neglected.

Real culture of the Individual has always consisted in the realization of the latent powers of man, in bringing these to light, in learning by experience how to use them. Hence arise self-knowledge, self-control, and a higher evolution.

It is not a mere technical, intellectual acquirement, the ability to define principles and formulate propositions. It rather consists in testing them out in actual experience; first by self-analysis to become familiar with the real self, its capacities and powers, its motives and aims in life; and having grasped and adjusted all these, then to start consciously, deliberately, determinedly, and intelligently, on "the road to the South," on the upward climb toward the Light.

"Possessions," with the great majority of individuals, mean something outward, in space and time; what we have, and, for the time hold, rather than what we are. The average idea of enjoyment is something altogether superficial and transient. It is found, or supposed to be found, in variety of sensations, emotions and feelings; in ringing the changes on these, till vitality fails, disillusion or satiety supervenes, and old age or death closes the play. Often the appetite remains, when vitality fails, and Faust rejuvenated, would run the same gauntlet again. The pity of it is that thousands of these victims of either satiety or Tantalus seem never to dream that there are other values, or anything else, or better, in life.

And yet there is not one of these faculties, capacities and powers that is useless, or, in itself, evil or degrading. They are, one and all, resources of the Individual Intelligence; tools for the day's work; materials for the building of the Temple; whereas, they most frequently are made the motive and the aim of life. They are means to a higher end, and not the end itself.

Without the latent passions, emotions, and feelings, man would be a mere mechanism. If all were mind, or mere intellect, there could be neither the creation nor the appreciation of beauty. Every work of art would be soulless; music might amuse the intellect by intricate chords and variations, like a colorless kaleidoscope, but it could never touch the heart nor elevate the soul.

Music and art, in the highest sense, through consonant vibrations in us, open the doors and windows of the soul, put us in touch and tune with the Infinite, and *then*, the real harmony begins. We live for the time in another world and return with a sigh and recover the bated breath, as though we had seen a vision beyond words. Music is an agent, a talisman, a means to an end. It strikes in us chords that lie at the foundation, the combinations that unlock the doors, and the "Imprisoned Splendor" wings in and out like the doves of Hesperides.

Blunt the passions, the feelings and the emotions by over-indulgence, by vice and dissipation, and the royal guests desert the banquet hall, the doors of the soul creak on their hinges; and in place of the "music of the spheres" you have a devil's dance, and the orgies of despair!

*Does it pay?* It all depends on *use*. Here lie the resources, the real possessions of man. Here lies the "Parable of the Talents."

Look at the profusion, the prodigality, the beneficence of Nature, Flowers and Fruit, Beauty and Bloom and Fragrance everywhere. Where there is no eye to see, no hand to pluck, Mother Nature delights in profusion, seemingly because she is made that way and cannot help it. And yet, in this little Rose-garden of ours—the Human Soul -we tramp down the flowers, plant loathsome weeds and poisons that kill and degrade and besot us, set up the tables of the money-changers, drive out the doves of Hesperides, and turn the temple into a shambles for wild beasts. "Nothing pays." "Let us curse God and—die!"

Is there not something after all in the *Measure of Values*, and in the inexorable *Law of Use*?

And who *constrains* us but *ourselves*?

Can God and Nature be so prodigal, noting even the sparrows fall, and yet disregard the children of men?

What our resources are we can never imagine till we draw upon and begin to utilize them as others have done throughout the ages.

The "average sinner," seemingly to justify or excuse his own failure, will not believe that any have ever achieved. *But there they stand* all down the ages! Ecclesiastics help the deception and keep up the illusion by calling it *Miracle* or "Special Providence," and so prevent man from entering his birthright, *to possess it*; and so we sell our birthright for a mess of pottage. It is like the dissipated, poverty-stricken spendthrift, who shuts his eyes and refuses to believe that any, by industry, economy, integrity and hard work have secured a competency. And so he cries, "Come on, boys! let's have another drink, and then rob this bond-holder, who has more than his share."

The Measure of Values, and the Law of Use *hold everywhere*, in every department of human life; and the question, "Does it pay?" is practical and scientific to the last degree, and no one can answer but ourselves. As we answer will be the results, and nothing but ourselves can change them.

We must realize that the human body, the organism of man, with all its faculties, capacities and powers, is but an *instrument* of the Individual Intelligence; and that every experience in life, every episode in our career, is like a day's work; perfecting the instrument for more and better work, if used rightly; till we advance from height to height of being; to larger and still larger and more glorious fields of work and experience.

There would seem to be no limit to this evolution, this upward and onward journey of the human soul. The more good work done, the larger the capacity and the broader the field opening before us. "From height to height the spirit walks."

The primary endowment of man is Life and conscious Intelligence, with the power to use both.

This would seem to be the only gratuity, and whether we regard it as a blessing or a curse, depends on how we regard and use them.

The great majority in all time, through ignorance or recklessness, seem to have misused them.

Hence sickness, disease, deformity, and degradation.

It is a wonderful thing—this Law of Normal Use—from which health, harmony, comfort, joy, growth, and development result, while misuse and abuse degrade and destroy.

Divinity seems to have put within the grasp of man's Intelligence (if he *chooses and wills*) an almost infinite range in power, variety and application, of that subtle and basic Principle of affinity, balance and equilibrium, that unites the atoms in a molecule, or a chemical substance; that law of attraction and repulsion—the Parallelogram of Force—that holds the planets in their orbits. Divinity seems to have taken man into council and offered him, not only the Kingdom of Nature, but the royal domain of his own soul, as a reward for co-operation and loyal service, on condition that he shall use wisely, intelligently, loyally, and kindly, and not misuse or abuse.

Is it *worth while*? Will it *pay*?

Nor is this all, beneficent as it seems. The whole journey of life on the physical plane here below is so designed and planned as to make the natural aging and decay of the physical body supplement, unfold and develop the Spiritual Body, through the right use of the faculties, capacities, and powers of the Human Soul—the Individual Intelligence.

These are aspects, uses and powers of that subtle *something* we call *Life*; that *Principle* that

"Runs through all time, extends through all extent,
Lives undivided, operates unspent."

Normal use that insures growth and development, range and power of action, is also, from first to last, a *refining* process; while misuse and abuse of these powers degrade and brutalize *inevitably*.

It follows, therefore, as the bodily structure and functions fail *under normal use* those of the spiritual body open, develop and unfold. First the seed, then the plant, then the flower and finally the fruit "of a well-spent life."

There is no "theory" or "guess-work" about it. It becomes, step by step, a matter of conscious, intelligent, individual experience. We know it just as we know that fire will burn or that we are here now, living, breathing, and acting.

If I thrust my finger into a flame, all the philosophers and metaphysicians of the world could not "argue" me out of the experience of the fact of "burn" and "pain"; nor could theologians succeed any better by quotations from Scripture! Man is so constituted that the *facts* of *experience* are stubborn things; and the more open to reason the individual the more convincing the facts of experience. Ignorance, superstition, and fear recede in the presence of these Lights of man's intelligence, as do dogma and despotism, that seek to enslave the human soul.

Theologians tell us that it is exceeding dangerous to take all this responsibility upon ourselves, thus appealing to ignorance, superstition, and fear.

I would answer: I refuse to take the responsibility of *disregarding* or *disobeying* the Law which the Divine and Universal Intelligence has placed at the *very foundation* of man's being; and I am so *un*orthodox as to imagine and believe that God knew what he was about, even better than the theologians, or the "Infallible" Italian who misinterprets God, Nature, and Man.

To-day, as I write, "God's Vicegerent" is instigating and promoting a "Holy War" in Priest-ridden Spain, over the temporal power of the Vatican, angered to the point of murder over the "posting of notices of places of public worship," other than Catholic.

They would rather turn the world into one "City of the Dead," than yield *one point* of Freedom, Enlightenment, or Self-government to man.

And men still call this *Religion*, and cast aside the crucifix for the sword, the gun and the firebrand. The *Inferno* has never yet been portrayed or even outlined. Its name is Priestcraft and Intolerance under the name of "Religion."

And is this a "Study in Psychology"? Yea, verily! Scientific Psychology is the only thing that goes to the very bottom of it, and defines and classifies every element, every fact in human experience. Man cannot build a *home* on a piece of ground where a slaughter-house disputes every square yard of ground with the tombstones of a graveyard. Clericalism is ever the one or the other, and frequently both; denying to man the right to build a *home* for himself anywhere, except by its permission and according to its plans and specifications, fixing the rent and the revenues for all future time.

The Premier of Spain to-day is disputing this prerogative of Rome, and the graveyard has been thrown open. The pity, the marvel of it all is, that the people generally do not seem to care, and call any statement of facts "sensational" or "panicky."

I am told by some very good people that these references to Popery seem irrelevant, and by others, that they mar the symmetry of my essay.

They are reminded that we are dealing with real and permanent values, and with what man may do and ought to do for himself.

Lying squarely across this upward pathway of man, to be pursued by free choice and personal effort, is the dogma of the Vicarious Atonement and the forgiveness of sin, of which "His Holiness" claims to hold the *exclusive agency.*

Through appeal to superstition and fear this preposterous and sacrilegious claim to-day, as in all the past, paralyzes the will and discourages the personal efforts of millions of men and women. Between that blind credulity which makes personal effort unnecessary, and the miracle and dogma which make it seem useless, the upward and onward march of man is hindered or annulled, notwithstanding the fact that many men and women lead noble lives who are yet communicants of the Church, both Catholic and Protestant. True, they may, with little thinking, reason and reflection from early education and "lip-service," give intellectual assent to these dogmas. But the lives they lead and the personal effort put forth prove them "better than their creeds." They say with the lips, "Christ has forgiven us," or "Jesus will save us," and while they are *saying* these things they *go to work saving themselves* by "leading the life" through personal effort and experience.

In other words, they "save themselves" in spite of their creeds and superstitions.

It is, therefore, with this exact "measure of values," that we are dealing; and the necessity and value of these considerations are nowhere so plain to-day, or so imperative, as just here, in the face of these demoralizing dogmas and pretensions of men, who contradict all natural law and steal unblushingly the prerogatives of God, as his "Vicegerent." The marvel of it is that it excites neither surprise nor protest, but is treated with a smile of good-natured complacency outside its circle of dupes.

He who treats it seriously, as a thing that, more than any other, demoralizes, discourages and paralyzes *millions*, is regarded as "sensational," "emotional," or an "alarmist."

In the face of all the facts, of which the daily papers are full, and the record of the Vatican crowded, I prefer that my own arraignment *shall stand*. No one who knows half these facts can dispute or gainsay them. We are making history here to-day, as mankind has had to make it in all the past, in the face of these "Lions in the path" of civilization and progress.

If I must choose between being superficial, ignorant and insincere, or being an "alarmist," I certainly and unhesitatingly choose to be an *alarmist*! The strongest ally of Superstition to-day is credulity, or indifference. The average man says, "I do not *believe* there is any danger"; and if he "spoke his heart" would add, "if there is, I do not *care*."

I would only reply, "If you mean to be honest, read, observe, and see." You may wait too long. Spain and Portugal are just awakening from the priest-ridden lethargy of centuries, and are making history anew. May a just God and all the angels help and protect them.

The great daily newspapers of the country are very conservative wherever Rome is concerned. She is too powerful and her resources too well organized and available to be disregarded.

It is therefore very significant that an editorial in one of the largest and most influential of these papers to-day gives a clear, concise, and impartial epitome of the "*Row in Spain*," clearly locating its cause and animus in the Vatican, and showing how unbearable this tyranny and exploitation had become to a large portion of the people of Spain.

I refer to this here for a special purpose, which involves and lies at the foundation of all other issues and considerations. And that is the statement in this editorial, that while the Church of Rome has held practically *undisputed sway* in Spain *for centuries*, with immense tracts of land, houses and revenues, independent of civil authority, with **20,000** priests, **5,000** communities with **60,000** inmates in a population of only **20,000,000** of people—*Seventy per cent. of the people are entirely uneducated.* With every opportunity, plenty of time and almost boundless resources, *Rome has kept the people in ignorance, the easier to rob them*; determined to *own* the land, the resources, and the people—body and soul—as the *Autocrat* of heaven and earth! A slavery in the name of "Religion" found nowhere else on earth to-day.

So much for Spain and the Vatican to-day. For the sequel, watch the daily papers.

And what has this to do with America? With Psychology? With the Measure of Values?

Simply this: Is anyone so dense as to suppose that the *Seventy per cent.* of dense ignorance in Spain is an accident, or an oversight of the Vatican and its servants? There lie the "policy" and the secret of the power of Rome.

In America our foundations, our bulwarks, and our hope and security of Freedom, Enlightenment, and Progress lie in our Free Public Schools. These Rome hates, condemns as "Godless," and would destroy if she could, as continually proved by the letters and edicts of the Popes.

Seeing, however, that she cannot do this, and fearful of losing her hold on her thirteen or fourteen million of communicants in America, she rushes the building of Parochial Schools, and threatens her people with dire penalties who patronize any other. Since she cannot *prevent* education here, as in Spain, she must "educate" *in her own way*, in order to retain her power over the rising generation. The basis of this education are ignorance, superstition, and fear; its crown, the slavery of conscience and the "Dogma of Obedience." The brutality of Ignorance in Spain is the sophistry of Priestcraft under the name of "Religion," in America.

The Genius of the Vatican is "Infallibility." It not only never errs, but it never changes. It dons another mask, adopts another slogan, and is now engaged in a great crusade to *educate*!

Constructive Psychology, the building of Individual Character, means the *precise opposite* of every principle, proposition, and practice of Popery. I desire to make this plain and unmistakable.

Nothing on earth transcends in importance this basic, universal, and *eternal antithesis*. It marks and monuments, in all time, the *Parting of the Ways* between Good and Evil; between Liberty and Despotism; between Light and Darkness; between Evolution and Devolution; between "Modernism" and Paganism; between Civilization and the Dark Ages; between the "Sermon on the Mount"—the Beatitudes, and the *Spanish Roman Vatican Inquisition*!

And this "antithesis," this issue, is as imminent, as active, as burning in America to-day, as it is in Spain. It only faces different ways.

Spain is *compelled* to redeem her *past*; America to guard and protect her *future*.

It is, from first to last, a Psychological Problem.

It is an analysis by fire, in the crucible of fate and destiny, to determine *accurately* the measure of values to the Individual, to Society, and to Civilization.

No man, woman or child, no society, no civilization ever has, or ever can, escape this issue.

It is the design on the trestle-board of Time.

It is the Modulus of both God and Nature regarding Man.

It is the Theorem of Psychology.

It involves the Evolution and Destiny of the Human Soul.

As civilization in many places showed an advancing tendency from the darkness, despotism and brutality of the Dark Ages, the "Robber Barons" began to disappear. Their slogan was, "He may seize who hath the power and he may hold who can." Serfdom also began slowly to recede. Popery and Priestcraft assumed the rôle of these Barons, changed the slogan from brute force (reserving that for emergencies) to "Divine Prerogative," "Infallibility" (later), and pagan mummeries in the name of "Religion."

*The result, to the common people, remained unchanged* to the present day—poverty, ignorance, and oppression.

Popery boasts that it never changes, never relents, nor forgives an enemy, nor forgets an injury, nor fails to "get even," like any brute, whenever she can. And this *Power* is not only the assumed custodian of the religion of Jesus, but stands in the place of it, as a substitute, and the world tolerates it in the name of *Religion*!

As a problem in Psychology, we have been considering the nature, use, and measure of values of the resources, faculties, capacities, and powers of man as an Individual Intelligence.

Facing opportunities, we have seen that there is a Law of Use and Responsibility which cannot be evaded.

Institutions and societies of men are, one and all, from first to last, under the same law. It is simply an aggregate, into which not a new principle enters, nor one principle is changed. The recognized and scientifically determined value of man to himself, is the measure of his value to the State.

The reverse proposition is equally true.

The value of any Institution to the individual, or to the State, must be measured and determined in the same way and under the same law.

It may thus be seen that Institutions, like Popery, are deeply involved in this Law of Use and Measure of Values. This is simply making use of, and putting in practice, these basic principles.

*Of what use to man*, measured by these scientific standards of value, are Popery and Priestcraft?

I answer unhesitatingly and unqualifiedly *An unmitigated Curse!*

This answer is justified by all history, and is as true and as exact to-day, up to the latest act and message from Rome, as it was during the horrors of the Inquisition; and there are evidence and specific statements to show that Rome would re-establish the "Holy Inquisition" to-day, *if she dared and had the power*.

It is this power, exercised through fear, on the basis of ignorance and superstition so instilled by what Popery calls "Religious Education," that prevents the majority of fourteen millions in America to-day, as everywhere and in all time, from exercising their prerogative and doing their duty as *Individuals*.

Is it not plain, therefore, how impossible it is to separate the Individual and the Social status?

Psychology and Sociology are departments of one Science, viz.: the Science of Man, Anthropology. Individuals and Institutions are under one law, one law of use, one measure of values.

He who ignores, evades, or belittles these plain issues and scientific principles, can settle with the law in his own time, though he cannot evade them always.

Note.—During the last week of the year **1910**, the daily papers announced that before the beginning of **1911** *every Priest in the Diocese* was required to take an oath to oppose and resist *Modernism* and to *obey* in all things the dictum and dogmas of His Holiness. As everyone knows that under the term *Modernism* is included all progress, investigation, and civilization condemned by the Vatican, everything that even questions the dogmas and despotism of Rome, the meaning of this required *oath* is plain.

It is doubtless renewed by reason of (among others) a book,—"Letters to His Holiness by a Modernist," which, written seemingly by a Priest, makes exceeding plain the meaning of Modernism and the relation of the Vatican thereto. The book marks an epoch in the close of the old year and the beginning of the new, and Rome has acted accordingly. She can delay the stream of progress as she has always done, but she cannot turn it backward. It will eventually overwhelm her.

# CHAPTER V

## SUMMARY AND CONCLUSIONS

The problem of the continued conscious life of man after the death of the physical body, concerns the *where* and the *how*, and does not, and need not, concern us at all now. It is, literally, an "after consideration."

Who and what man is, here and now, is the real problem. Only when, or in the degree in which, we master this problem, can we really know anything definitely of the other.

The complete separation of these two problems, and the exact definition and formulation of each, is the first step on the road to knowledge of the Science of the Soul.

For the time being, in the study of Psychology, "other worldliness" should be absolutely abandoned.

Almost everyone finds it difficult to do this. Many find it impossible.

The fear and uncertainty with which almost everyone faces the inevitable, the loss of friends, the broken lute, the empty chair, the lonely life—all these make us cry out in anguish—*where* and *how* and *when*, and overlook the "*what are we?*"

So-called Religion in all time has almost hopelessly mixed and confused these problems.

The various concepts and doctrines of rewards and punishments hereafter, have put ulterior motives in the place of actual values, weakened the will and hindered man from doing his best.

A still further confusion follows, in the measure of assets, that leads to time-serving and false values.

Satisfy the average individual that "death ends all" and he will cry, "Let us eat, drink, and be merry, for to-morrow we die," notwithstanding the fact that he sees others who have "gone the pace," realized only "dust and ashes," declared it "all a mistake," and that if they had the chance they would "do it all the other way."

Remember, we are dealing with *actual values* here and now, divested of both fear and anticipation of the hereafter.

On the other hand, who ever saw an individual die, who had led a clean, upright, kindly life, indulge in regret or remorse, or declare life a disappointment or a failure?

The first is anchored to the physical plane by insatiate appetite and passion, or desire to reform, which might soon be forgotten.

The other has found sweetness and joy in life, in conscious growth, in doing good; and his soul is illumined and transfigured as the body fails and he approaches another plane, and this often independent of any formulated religious belief.

It all depends on what the man is *within* himself, his intrinsic character, his *real self*; and no matter where he goes, that character, that self, goes with him. It *is* Himself.

The "change in a moment, in the twinkling of an eye," is not in the *man* and cannot be. It is in the plane, or sphere, or world he inhabits, or to which he goes. It is a change of garments, of habitat, of houses in which we live—if we live at all.

This much we *know*, and should not forget or confuse it. We know it, as we know that "twice two are four"; that fire will burn, or that bodies, unsupported, fall to the ground. We know it from the fact of our own self-conscious identity. Radically or suddenly to change that essentially is to annihilate *us*.

The preacher says, "Study the Bible." He might say, "Study yourself!" The preacher says, "Look to Jesus." He might say, "Look within!" The preacher says, "Repent and pray." I would say, "After an inventory of your inner possessions, clean up the house and *go to work* to improve it in every way."

When "cleaning day" is well under way, if the "sure-enough" preacher drops in, and you show him the house and what you are trying your best to do, he will just start "Old Hundred," and will be too happy for anything else.

I am not criticising the preacher, nor opposing religion, but getting ready for it, laying the foundation of Morals and the building of character. "Religion" cannot do this. *You* and *I* have to do it, or it is never done.

Without this work of *ours*, religion is little more, or else, than passing emotion or lasting superstition, "lip service," cant, hypocrisy, and then cold heartless dogmatism, a measure and jingling of words that never touch the heart, but leave the individual ready to throw stones and light brands of torture: a case-hardening of the affections and the aspirations, that wraps the soul like the bandages of the mummied Pharaohs, a mere petrifaction.

We know, or may know, as much actually and scientifically of the growth of the soul as of the growth of the body. The average individual knows more of the soul than of the body, but his knowledge is in confusion. It is a matter of hourly, daily, life-long, and changing *experience*. He knows little of physiology, except feelings, sensations, desires, and results. How and why the mechanism of the body works he knows not.

Body and soul are organically identified, intimately associated and interwoven, and act and react on each other. They are functionally synchronous in all movements. The analogies between them are numberless and easily traced.

The physician and physiologist does not stop to inquire, "What *is* Life" and refuse to move till someone gives a satisfactory answer; yet he is dealing with Life in its numberless manifestations in the human, organism continually.

But this same physician is likely to debate and deny the existence of the Soul, demanding that you define and demonstrate it.

The term "Individual Intelligence" is as definite, specific, and demonstrable in Psychology as the term "Life" in Physiology.

We are alive and we possess a certain degree or measure of intelligence. These are facts in our conscious experience.

We may shape or mold our lives. We may do this according to our ideals, or we may drift with the tides of circumstance, or of passion and caprice, and this is what most persons do.

So also with that intelligence which is the guiding light in our lives. It may illumine our pathway, or it may flash and fitfully glare, with the shadows, rendering our pathway obscure and uncertain, illusory and deceitful, or dangerous and fearful.

The soul is in the body; and this light of intelligence is in the soul, its center, its very essence.

All else in us, and round about us, is diversity and multiplicity. This light of intelligence in us is *One* and unchanging.

Our experience in life, however varied and diversified, is co-ordinated and unified by this Intelligence in us. It is that which puts all our experiences together and views them through a single lens. It stands by itself alone, and all else pays tribute to it.

It is the pronoun "I" and it stands for, speaks and acts for, all else in us.

It is not alone the only *unity* in us, but it is that which unifies all the rest, uses the "possessive case," and may subordinate all else in us to its Will.

Does it, then, do violence to common sense and hourly experience, or is it any stretch of the imagination to speak of this unity as an entity, and call it the human soul?

If we live after the change called death, in a spiritual world, in place of the physical we now inhabit, and with a spiritual or refined body to correspond with that plane of refined or etherialized substance, the Individual Intelligence must function in that body and on that plane as it does now in the physical body on the physical plane.

Either something very like this takes place, or we cease to exist as a self-conscious individual intelligence. There must remain and continue man's self-conscious identity.

Furthermore, if this be true, the *real nature* of this individual intelligence we call the *Self*, in the last analysis, is likely to be as much a mystery as ever. We may know *who we are* without knowing *what it is*.

Now the composite nature of man, as we know it, not only justifies all these analogies, but seems to show that the modulus, the germ at least, of the spiritual body exists now within the physical; that it does not disintegrate when the physical body dies, but separates and coheres more closely than ever; and is still inhabited or possessed by the individual intelligence.

Moreover, it has often been seen by clairvoyants at the time of death, thus verifying the Biblical declaration, "there is a natural (physical) body, and there is a spiritual body."

The composite structures of man's organism above referred to are well known. They are called "systems." The bony or Osseous system, the muscular system, the circulatory system, the lymphatic system, and the two nervous systems, serve as illustrations of the composite nature of man.

All of these "systems" more or less inter-penetrate and diffuse each other.

There is also a chemico-vital, kinetic, or magnetic body, diffused through and inter-penetrating all the rest. This gives the contrast between the living organism (with the flush of health upon the cheek and the light of intelligence in the eyes), and a corpse.

Death is often instantaneous, while decomposition often waits for days.

There is a still further analogy regarding a single function, like a sensory or motor impulse, passing to or from the central brain, the organ of consciousness. The journey is one of relays and orderly sequences.

This is proven in a great variety of forms of paresis. I cannot, as an individual intelligence, *directly* move my hand any more than I can move a mountain. I conceive the object or act and set the will in motion. The impulse traverses the nerves, is transferred to the muscle, and then, when the circuit is complete, *I* move my hand.

The gap between my conscious intelligent wish and will, and my physical hand, is very great. One is metaphysical, the other physical. There is, therefore, a point of correlation where the one is converted into the other.

The knowledge of these facts, and of this orderly sequence and correlation, constitutes the Science of pathology and enables us to locate the lesion or disease. I cannot move my hand, and the pathologist locates the "short-circuit" in brain, or nerve, or "terminal plate," or muscle, as the case may be.

Now it is this *system* of *composite systems* that deserves special attention. We know that it exists as a series of relays and refining processes. In disease it is interrupted, or out of joint, or broken down.

Health means harmony, concord, rhythm between every part, and the power of the one individual intelligence to use it all, to act or refrain from action, and to hold and maintain through all, repose, equilibrium, and self-mastery.

The physical body we know to be a thing of sense and time. We know its beginning, its gestation, its entrance and exit on this material plane. Its secrets are all involved in the subtle relations it bears to the soul that inhabits, unifies, and utilizes it.

The Individual Intelligence, Ego, Soul, or Entity, is as patent to us in our *awareness of self* as is the body it inhabits. It is our *very self.* Our knowledge of it is a *direct personal experience*, so direct, immediate, and constant that we overlook its significance.

I can see no reason to imagine that a human being, passing from the earthly plane and consciously living on the spiritual plane and recognizing itself as the same individual, would be any wiser as to the exact nature and origin of the Individual Intelligence than he is now; though his field of vision and range of conscious experience had so immeasurably increased and expanded.

If he had solved this problem of *ultimates*, he would be at the end of his thread of life and would compass the Infinite. He would be no longer Man, but God.

So, from all these considerations, and from all directions, we come back to human evolution, the upward and onward journey of the human soul.

As man's health, usefulness, and happiness here depend on the perfection and utility of the physical body he inhabits, and its maintenance in health and harmony, have we the least reason to imagine that the same individual, dwelling on the spiritual plane, will not be under the same of analogous laws and relations there, since we have assumed the persistence and conscious identity of the soul there as here?

I hold, therefore, that man possesses, now and here, the structure of a *Spiritual* Body; and that the "growth of the soul" and our status and relation to the soul, and our status and relation to the life after death on the spiritual plane, depend *very largely* on the character and integrity of this spiritual body, the "house we have builded."

The whole of life, therefore, here, is what gestation of the infant body is before birth. When the child is born it is a separate personality, a distinct individuality.

There has been woven into its organism a distinct and synchronous correspondence with that of the mother.

During gestation it has passed through every plane of organic life, from *amœba*, or mollusk, to man.

It is thus in touch with every phase and quality of life. It epitomizes them all, transcends them all, and *may co-ordinate* them all.

On the other hand, the individual intelligence of the child, a distinct and separate *unity*, is in vital, spiritual, and synchronous relation to that of the mother that enfolds it.

It is either building or rejuvenating a new spiritual body, as the "essential form" of the physical, organic, chemical, and kinetic or magnetic body.

What we call "Life," or "Vitality," runs like a "dominant chord" in the harmonic scale of the whole. Each part, organ, and function is related to every other and to the whole by definite vibrations and the laws of harmony.

If, from the beginning, it is an "unwelcome child," the higher and subtler elements of the mother's nature, and all her emotions are turned against it, are discordant and not constructive and harmonic.

Discord is thus ingrained at the foundations and woven into the "subtle body" of the child.

Nature is so persistent in its determination to preserve and perpetuate the human race, that the building of the organic body of the child goes on; and the Individual Intelligence is so potent that it often triumphs over these prenatal obstructions, but by no means always. If "there *is* a spiritual body" in the mother organism during the present life, as I am *entirely satisfied* there is; and if the child is laying the foundation and weaving the pattern and fabric of a spiritual body of its own for the present life and that immediately beyond; then these psychological influences and conditions are of *transcendent importance* and *may* be largely determined by our intelligent choice.

A higher race of beings will never inhabit this earth till these fundamental laws are recognized and regarded.

We may illustrate and symbolize this spiritual habitation we are building by the over-tones and the harmonics in music.

Its nature and function and the whole process of building and development are a refining and purifying process.

It may be conceived in the vito-magnetic field of man, as that which is in nearest relation and closest touch with the soul, the Individual Intelligence, and through, and by which the soul acts.

Being in synchronous relation with the physical organs and functions, like a chord in music, a high with a lower tone (but still harmonic), the *direct* vehicle and agent of the soul would be this spiritual body; and when the physical body or vehicle dies, or is cast off, the spiritual body *with the soul* escapes.

Empirical evidence along just these lines is so abundant in the annals of every people, and in all ages, that it is unnecessary to quote it here. Whole volumes are filled with it, outside the annals of Spiritualism and the Psychical Society, and antedating them by centuries and millenniums.

The most important consideration is that the building of character by voluntary choice and personal effort, the "growth of the soul," and the evolution of this spiritual body are *inseparable*. This trinity which is man, is *potentially* (and may be *actually*) a *unity*.

The evolutionary and devolutionary lines run in precisely opposite directions, are easily differentiated and defined, are usually recognized by observation and by the individual himself. It is very difficult and takes a long time to deceive ourselves with regard to the upward or downward trend of our own life, till we have blunted by misuse and degraded all the finer faculties, capacities, and powers of our being.

A quickened conscience, a moral uplift, a desire to do right, a noble ideal, mark the beginning; but self-study, a rigid and persistent self-analysis, taking account of stock of all our resources and capacities, all our real possessions and opportunities, is the scientific process by which man may become master of his own life and evolve to higher and still higher planes of being, even here in the present life.

The question of rewards and punishments hereafter, and what we may expect, or hope, or fear, that we will *get*, will sink into utter nothingness before the great and ever-

70

growing question of what we *are*, and what we are determined to *become*.

Incidentally with this dominating impulse and determination will be the growth and development of the spiritual body, and the intuition and guiding light of the Individual Intelligence. We shall become consciously *aware* of this as a constant personal experience demanding no further proof. It is *knowledge* of the soul *direct*.

Every faculty, capacity, and power of the soul will be our willing servant.

This is Constructive Psychology, and is a normal evolution under both Natural and Divine Law: "Living the Life that we may know the doctrine."

It is practical, scientific Psychology worked out and demonstrated in the Laboratory of Life. Religions and Revelations will no longer be mysteries, but open books; for we shall be in touch with their source and at-one with their inspiration.

This is what is meant by "The School of Natural Science."

Nor is it an idle speculation, nor merely a thing "devoutly to be wished."

If the whole nature of man is built and operated under law; if he is, as he seems to be, an aggregate of all substances, an epitome of all principles and processes; then it follows that to understand these laws, processes and correspondences, is to become *master* of them and of life.

Wonderful as have been the discoveries in nature's finer forces and in applied science, all that science has discovered or invented, or art has devised, is like children's toys, when compared with the subtle and marvelous mechanism of man's organism.

The rhythmic beating of the heart, synchronous with respiration and the circulation of the blood, are sufficient illustrations. But even this concerns the vehicle, not the driver; the instrument, not the player upon this "harp of a thousand strings."

When it comes to the mental and psychical realm, cognition is direct and immediate. We become "aware" of relations and processes, of sequences and powers, by intuition, as we are *aware* of the Self.

This is *apperception* in its highest sense. Not through the mind, which is a *process* and a function, but through that which uses, controls and dominates the mind, viz.: the Individual Intelligence, the Soul.

In the mind, in daily life, *we* weigh and measure, reason, choose, compare, and adjust. In intuition or apperception it is borne in, or comes like a flash of light, and seems as if "we always knew it."

We may somewhat haltingly describe the process, but we can never impart the knowledge to another, because it is an *individual experience*. As easily could another feel, sense, and *realize* the pain of thrusting our finger into the fire, as to receive vicariously, from us, a *real* physical experience.

Here lies the difficulty, often the impossibility, of the teacher or the Master, in imparting his knowledge.

I am *entirety satisfied* that by personal effort and experience along these lines of normal higher evolution, there comes a time and a degree of unfoldment and power when, from knowledge and self-mastery, the Master—the Individual Intelligence—having evolved and learned to *control* the spiritual body, can consciously and deliberately pass out of the physical body and return to it at will. He can do this as consciously and completely as it occurs at death; can go where he pleases, within the range of his unfoldment or spiritual experience, and retain conscious memory of it all after his return to the physical body.

And suppose this all to be true, how can he demonstrate the fact, or transmit the experience to another; and particularly if that other declared to begin with that, "the whole process is absurd and impossible"?

Nor is mere credulity here a highway to knowledge. It is merely the opposite pole of incredulity, and both are begotten by ignorance.

Analogy and the basic principles and laws of scientific psychology are very different matters indeed. They point in this direction like a theorem in mathematics. The principles and laws being grasped and apprehended, the solution becomes only a question of *work*; and at every step the law is verified, "Backward and forward it still spells the same."

What is this but the *methods* of Natural Science applied to Psychical Science upon the basis of the Unity of Natural Phenomena and Universal Law?

There is nothing to prevent any of us from starting on this upward journey of the soul, if we choose; and never till we do, shall we really begin to *know*, to realize our birthright, and progress toward the realm of eternal day.

The science of ethics, the basis of morals, is the starting point, the first step; and *leading the life*, the way. And there is no climbing up some other way. So said the Master of Galilee, and so say the real Masters in all times.

When Jesus said, "I am the Way, the Truth, and the Life," he doubtless meant that these were all *in him*, and he at-one with them.

When Jesus said, "I and the Father are *one*. No one cometh to the Father but by me," he doubtless referred to this at-one-ment as the only way by which the natural man—Adam—could become the Spiritual man—*Christos*.

When he said, "The kingdom of heaven is within you," he undoubtedly meant that "heaven" is a condition, a harmonic state, and not a place.

We undoubtedly create our own "hell" and our own "heaven," and people them with "devils" or with "angels."

True Science and true Religion clasp hands, and are like the two hands of the one body of Truth. They check each other, supplement each other, harmonize each other.

Superstition and blind dogma are the enemies of true Science; Religion—never.

Science and Religion are the handmaids of Truth; because both are the children of Divinity, the agents of Light and of Eternal Progress for Man.

This building of character, this growth of the soul, this Harmonic of Evolution, is a matter of *work*; of personal endeavor, of valid, real, personal experience.

Its results are our *real* possessions, our "treasure in heaven" that nothing can ever destroy. Life and Death may ebb and flow, and come and go; but *we* may, if we will, go on forever; or we may turn the other way and go down to death. *Some day* every human soul will elect, choose, and decide and then start on the journey, North or South.

This is the meaning of Soul, of Individual Intelligence, of Rational Volition, of Personal Responsibility.

It is the Science of Nature aligned with Divinity, and compassing Humanity.

The purpose of these outlines, suggestions, analogies, and inferences, is to show that this life is a period of gestation, in close analogy and comparable with that of the child *in utero*; that with the web and woof of character, organ and function, impulse and use, opportunity and destiny, we are building a spiritual body, the *immediate vehicle* of the soul, as literally as is the physical body on the outer material plane; that the laws of Spiritual health and vitality are as concrete, apprehensible, and demonstrable as those of physiology.

Normal use under law develops health, harmony, and strength, in the one case as in the other, demonstrably; and these laws, accurately formulated and demonstrated, constitute the School of Natural Science, accessible to all prepared to receive and wisely use them; advancement depending on progress, thoroughness, and loyalty, in all preceding degrees.

Is it worth while?

# CHAPTER VI

## THE CROSS IN RELIGION AND THE CRUX IN SCIENCE WITH THE GREAT WORK IN AMERICA

With the progress of civilization and the general growth and diffusion of intelligence everywhere, there is one problem upon which all else focalizes, though the fact seems to be seldom clearly apprehended or realized.

Not only do science and religion face each other at one point, but the life of each is at that one point involved. It is not only the often recognized "conflict between Religion and Science," which was long ago worn threadbare. It is the fact that both Science and Religion are out of joint with themselves.

The battle-ground may, in a broad way, be named Psychology. All problems and all discussions of the real issues arise from, involve, or center around, the nature, laws that govern, and destiny of the Human Soul.

From the very nature of these problems, their intricacy and diversity, they remained the latest in the categories of Science to be seriously investigated.

For the same reasons they have been the subject of dogma and revelation in religion, with doors slammed in the face of all investigation as not only useless, but wicked, and often made dangerous.

Between the agnosticism of Science, and the dogmatism of Religion, knowledge has been crucified, and there it hangs to-day, a crux to the one, and the Cross to the other: The same problem, only facing different ways.

And yet the Reconciliation is not far to seek. It is difficult for the average churchman, or theologian, to apprehend and remember, that a *fact*, in nature or in life, is one thing; and that the *interpretation*, or *explanation* put upon that fact, by any man, or body of men, is another thing entirely. Here is where Belief, Dogma, and Heresy come in. As soon as one denies the interpretation, he is accused of denying the fact, no matter how illogical or absurd the interpretation may be, on the one hand, or how openly he admits the fact as the basis of his own conclusions, on the other.

Few individuals will be found nowadays who deny the *fact* of the birth, life, mission, and death of Jesus of Nazareth. But the interpretations read into the fact differ so widely as to result in almost numberless sects, and an endless war of words. All this theological wrangling may be focalized at one point, almost on a single word. Did Jesus of Nazareth differ in kind or in *Degree*, from the rest of Humanity?

If he had "a like nature with ours," as he and his disciples took the utmost pains to declare, and to demonstrate, then he differed in *degree* of unfoldment, and was indeed, our Elder Brother; He differed as the holy differs from the unholy; as the pure differs from the impure; as the kind and charitable differ from the unkind and the uncharitable. It is just at this point that all the theological juggling comes in, in the effort to reconcile contradictions and irreconcilable paradoxes, under the designation—Mystery, Miracle, and Faith. Few theologians would admit that it is desirable, even if possible, that the mystery and miracle should disappear, and that wisdom and understanding should take their place. In other words, that Jesus should be proved an evolution under both natural and divine law, as the result of "Living the Life."

Bear in mind that we are dealing with *Interpretations* only, and with the opinions of men; and that there is nothing "sacred" or "holy" about these opinions, no matter how they may be hedged about by dogma, or ecclesiastic authority. The Immaculate Conception; the Virgin Birth; the Resurrection of the physical body, and the Vicarious Atonement, are each and all Dogmas; the opinions of men, in *interpreting* the mystery, and miracle, they have assigned to the nature of Jesus, in what they call the "plan," or the "Scheme of Salvation."

If the nature of Jesus were radically and essentially different from ours; if he differed from us in *kind*, instead of in *degree*; if he were "very God," instead of a perfected man, as the result of "Living the Life"; then he can have little in common with us; and, so far as "like natures," "common temptations," and human sympathies, and destinies, are concerned, he might as well have been born on the planet Mars.

But suppose that psychic and spiritual science could so define the faculties, capacities, and powers of man, and the nature and laws of the human soul, as to demonstrate the fact that Jesus became *Christos* through "living the life," and "doing the will of the Father," in strict conformity to both Natural and Divine Law, thus revealing the fact that these *potencies* are *latent* in every human soul: that it does not depend so much upon what we *believe*, as upon what we *do*; not so much upon what we *profess*, as upon what we *are*; not so much upon what Jesus did for us, as upon what we do for ourselves and for others, in strict analogy with the life and the teachings of Jesus. Would not Jesus become, indeed and in truth, a *Living Example*, in place of a "Blood Offering"?

Theology ignores and sophisticates *Personal Responsibility*, which everything else, and every experience in life, justifies and enforces as the basis of Morals.

On the other hand, so-called Psychic Science misapprehends, belittles, and sophisticates the Human Will, the prime Motor Power of Man. It then confuses Rational Volition and Domination by juggling with the words *Suggestion* and *Hypnosis*.

This reveals the fact that they have no rational concept whatever of the psychical nature of man, not even a "working hypothesis" of the Human Soul. Theologians affirm, "Science" denies, and so they still face each other in this Twentieth Century with "A war of words," though, to a considerable extent, they have ceased making faces and calling each other names, because there is a deeper struggle going on.

The Theological Hierarchy, worldly-wise in every generation, has dropped the cry of *Heresy* and gone to the very foundations of our civilization. They are sapping and mining the foundations of civil Liberty, the "self-evident truths," and the "Inalienable Rights," upon which this government was founded.

Here is a thoroughly-organized, relentless determination, openly declared, and well under way to destroy our "Free Public Schools," and substitute that "Organized Ignorance," the Parochial Schools, as the first step in reuniting Church and State, through dogmatic authority instilled into the youths of this country. Not one citizen in a thousand seems to realize what is here being attempted, how thoroughly organized it is, or what immense progress in this direction has already been made; or, if they know, they do not seem to care.

It may thus be seen what practical and vital issues we are facing and how much is involved in the "Cross of Religion," and the "Crux of Science."

Intelligence, Education, the Light of Science, and the Illumination of true Religion, are pitted in a conflict with Ignorance, Superstition, and Fear; dogmatism, degeneration, and devolution.

Science and Religion represent different departments in human interests and the life of man. So far as they are each true, they must eventually, and inevitably clasp hands, instead of working at cross-purposes.

Actual knowledge of the human soul, as a Science of psychology, on the one hand; and the duty of man to himself, to his fellows, and to God, and the destiny of the human soul as essential religion, on the other; must constitute the basis of union, and the point of agreement.

The accredited psychology of to-day has hitherto failed to demonstrate any actual knowledge of the human soul, or even to postulate its existence, as a fact in nature.

The theologies and religions of to-day appeal largely to superstition and fear, and support their dogmas by "revelations," the diverse interpretations of which have segregated religions into a large number of sects with no bond of union or basis of agreement.

Competition here, in securing proselytes, differs little, except in name, from that everywhere in evidence between commercial organizations. It is hardly "the survival of the fittest," but rather, as everywhere, and in all ages, the triumph of the most powerful, aggressive, and unscrupulous. The Roman Hierarchy is still in the lead, with its Pope "infallible," and anathematizing all progress and enlightenment, under the designation of "Modernism," and all its energy exerted to perpetuate the "Dark Ages."

It is thus that priestcraft masquerades in the name of religion to enslave the human soul. Still outside this Babel of religion and science, lie numberless cults and organizations professing both liberty and enlightenment along the lines of man's spiritual nature, not one of which puts forth any *clear and definite theorem* of the human soul. With mere assertions, instead of demonstrated facts, and appealing often to the desire for wealth, health, and comfort in their followers, they often declare that one has only to "*demand*" these things, in order to have them. Justice and the law of compensation are often entirely ignored, and the methods employed are *un*moral, to say the least, almost without exception, unscientific, and wholly empirical.

Occasionally we find "Leaders," or "Official Heads," whose colossal ignorance of either moral or spiritual Law, is only equaled by their monumental egotism, and this does not prevent them from gaining proselytes, and amassing fortunes in their own name.

It would be difficult to see how many of these cults differ, either in principle or practice, or in the results wrought out in their disciples, from the Priestcraft already referred to.

They advertise an open thoroughfare, and seem to promise something for nothing, but from the vicarious atonement, up or down the scale, the votaries pay in "mint, anise, and cummin," while ignorantly blind to the weightier matters of the law.

To one who for half a century has studied these personal and social problems, and witnessed the rise and fall of many of these cults, from the Fox Sisters and Spiritualism, to Braid and Hypnotism, while Priestcraft and Popery, like Tennyson's brook, "go on forever," it all seems pitiful that mankind must pay so dearly for freedom, enlightenment, and knowledge.

And yet, when the real teacher comes, the rabble so long exploited cry, "Away with him," "Crucify him." When the rabble at last repent, Priestcraft shifts its tactics and deifies the sacrifice, which it instigated, and so perpetuates the eternal tragedy.

Those familiar with the "Seeking after God," and for real knowledge of the essential nature of man, in all ages, are aware that there have always been, in every age, those who have achieved it. It has been known, or rather concealed, under many names. Its possessors and teachers have been reviled, persecuted, crucified, and thus their work has been hindered and often defeated.

The ignorant and superstitious feared it. The vicious, ambitious, and time-serving hated it, because it prevented the few from dominating and exploiting the many; liberating, as it does, the earnest seeker after truth and enlightenment from the bondage of ignorance, dogma, superstition, and fear, in every form.

Hence Institutional Religions, Schools of Philosophy, Coteries, Syndicates, and many other organizations of men, constituted to dominate and rule the masses, have been the sworn foes of individual liberty and enlightenment, and of the "Illuminati," or real teachers in every age, and a perpetual menace to their work.

Real knowledge of the nature and destiny of man, has first to be discovered, then recovered, and possessed. To become available, it must be simplified, formulated, and finally promulgated in some form, so as to reach those ready and capable of receiving it.

It must be sought earnestly and deservedly. The candidate must demonstrate that he is duly and truly prepared, worthy, and well qualified. Every step in advance is determined by his understanding and use of what he has hitherto received.

The real possession of this sublime wisdom is an evolution from within and not something communicated from without.

It is, literally, the building of character and the growth of the soul, as the highway of knowledge.

To discover, possess, exemplify, and promulgate this knowledge, this higher evolution of the Individual Intelligence, in the face of all obstacles and difficulties, has been known and designated for ages as the *Magnum Opus*, the "Great Work." It is, indeed, the greatest work either known, permitted or possible to man. It solves the riddle of the Sphinx of Life and makes Man Master of his own destiny.

Such a Master lives in a new world, untrammeled by the things of sense and time. He has indeed, "lived the life to know the doctrine," and can say with Jesus, in sincerity and truth, "I, and the Father, are One," because we are *at-one*.

There is not a particle of evidence in history, in philosophy, or in science, to show that anyone has ever reached such knowledge, liberation, and enlightenment, in any other way than that in which Jesus attained it; viz.: by renouncing the ordinary ambitions of life, wealth, fame, and power, and by overcoming selfishness and the lusts of the flesh; devoting their lives to the good of mankind, "without the hope of fee or reward." As the whole work is a spiritual unfoldment, and from beginning to end a refining process, it is easy to see how and why the conditions are what they are, and have always been the same.

This is why those who have no apprehension or conception of the process, can see only mystery and miracle in the result.

If anyone cites the so-called "black magicians" of Egypt, and of antiquity, to refute the moral code as the essential condition of attainment, they will find that these priests and "magi climbing up some other way," and whom Jesus designated as "thieves and robbers," could never function or pass beyond the so-called "astral plane." Here is where the Sibyl and the "virgin seer" came in.

This is clearly shown in that little book "The Idyll of the White Lotus," as in several of Bulwer's novels. Hypnotism and Ceremonial Magic, as revealed in the writings of Abbé Constant, represent ambition for knowledge and power without "living the life," and at any cost to mankind. These *Margraves* have often existed, sealed their own fate, and "gone to their own place." H. P. Blavatsky referred to them as "lost souls," or "soulless individuals." They are also graphically described in "The Strange Story of Arinzeman."

There was always the "Right-hand Path," and the "Left-hand Path."

Even a slight familiarity with ancient literatures and philosophies reveals the fact, that all these things have been known for ages. The subtlety of the Hindoo mind has been such as to leave no phase of mental or psychic phenomena uninvestigated.

To the casual and uninstructed reader, it often seems like an endless and hopeless jungle, and he is unable to bring order out of the seemingly endless confusion.

There is not a single percept or concept in what is now called "New Thought," that may not be found repeated with almost endless variations thousands of years ago.

Reference has already been made to the conditions imposed upon the student who aspires to know, and to become.

The obligations upon the teacher are no less stringent, for both are, from first to last, working under both natural and spiritual law to which they are bound to conform.

To be possessed of such knowledge the teacher must have abandoned worldly ambition, the love of wealth, and the applause of men. All motives of time-serving and self-seeking must assail him in vain. He becomes the almoner of the treasure-house of Light and Knowledge. He must exemplify what he teaches. If he can impart his knowledge, or assist an aspiring and worthy brother, it must be in the way he has himself received it, "without money and without price," or any "hope of reward or fee," and the brother so receiving, in his own degree, must be ready to pass it on under precisely the same terms and conditions.

The teacher, therefore, must be in a position to give or to withhold; promulgate or conceal; teach or refuse to teach; governed solely by Truth and Law, and the solemn obligation under which he has himself received it.

The meaning of the saying, "strait is the gate and narrow is the way, and few there be who find it," may thus be made apparent.

Fragments of this wisdom are found scattered through the ages, with here and there one who has achieved it.

For two or three centuries the early Christian Church undertook to work on these lines, and instituted three degrees, as abundantly shown in the  writings of many of the so-called "Christian, or Church Fathers."

Jesus said to his disciples, "I have many things to say unto you, but ye cannot bear them now." And again, "The works that I do, ye shall do also, and greater things than these shall ye do, because I go to the Father." And again, "Unto you it is given to know the mysteries of the kingdom of heaven, but to them who are without, it is not given."

Mysteries, indeed, to the ignorant monks who were already wrangling over creed, and dogmas, and who, in  at the First Council at Nice, fought it out surrounded by the soldiers of the Pagan Emperor, Constantine; and thus settled the "orthodox *interpretation*," of what they were wholly incompetent to understand. Their successors are still engaged in the same wrangle of interpretation, so far as the "Infallible Pope," and dogma of obedience, at Rome has been unable to suppress it.

Somewhere between the middle of the first and second centuries, an effort at union and reconciliation arose from another quarter. Ammonius Saccas, a Neo-Platonist, endeavored to unite men of different cults and beliefs on the lines of the Great Work, precisely as the Philalethean Society is doing in New York to-day; but his movement was soon engulfed and lost sight of by the tide of Ecclesiasticism, or suppressed by the soldiers of Constantine.

I am not attempting a history, for that would  fill volumes. I am only giving a few sidelights of the Great Work.

In the Tenth Century, at Baghdad, a society was formed admitting Jews, Christians, Mohammedans, and atheists, with a similar purpose.

During the time of Martin Luther, John Reuchlin made a similar attempt. Both Reuchlin and Luther were pupils of Trithemius, the Abbot of St. Jacob's at Würzburg, one of whose books I possess, printed in the year , and also another book, "The Theosophical Transactions of the Philadelphian Society," printed in London in . Browning's "Paracelsus" gives a splendid outline of the philosophy and teachings of Trithemius, and rescues Paracelsus with all who can understand, from the vile slanders of his monkish enemies; and Robert Browning wrote his "Paracelsus" at the age of twenty-three! Can you wonder why so few "understand Browning"?

For more than fifteen hundred years mankind has been involved between the speculations of Philosophy, on the one hand, and the creeds and dogmas of Theology, on the other.

There was also the deliberate destruction of ancient monuments, scrolls, and records, by religious fanatics. Diocletian, in A.D. , burned the books of the Egyptians.

Cæsar burned , Rolls at Alexandria, and Leo Isaurus , at Constantinople in the eighth century. Then came the Mohammedans, who destroyed the remainder of the accessible scrolls at Alexandria. Gangs of fanatical Monks, Christian and Pagan, roamed over Europe destroying and defacing everything upon which they could lay their hands, as witnesses against their dogmas and superstitions. Even to-day, in India, it is difficult for Europeans to gain access to genuine ancient records. The records of these barbarities are still fresh in the minds of the guardians of sacred lore.

Even with such a record for thousands of years, Ecclesiasticism is as arrogant and rampant as ever to-day. The wonder is, that there is anything left but barbarism.

Two writers declare that the most ancient and valuable of the records of the Alexandrian Library were kept in secret crypts known only to the highest officials, and preserved still in secret crypts known only to the Illuminati. In Baalbec and all through the East to-day these underground temples are being explored, and even the fragments found excite wonder and admiration. Ignorant Barbarians may be destructive on general principles, but fanatical Ecclesiasticism has ever been destructive of all light, knowledge and civilization, through insane hatred or pure "cussedness"! We need only to regard intelligently what it has done, and is doing for Southern Europe to-day.

Can you wonder that the real science of the Human Soul found little recognition, or that it was denied as possible to man?

As already shown, the Science of to-day has neither recognized nor worked up to it; and the Theology of to-day covers it with fable, mystery, and miracle as of old.

In spite of both these the "Philalethean Society" exists, the "Seekers after God" were never more numerous than now, and the *Magnum Opus*, the Great Work, was never, in the whole history of man, more in evidence than it is to-day.

"Truth crushed to Earth shall rise again,
The Eternal years of God are hers."

Can it be that there is no great truth back of all these struggles and aspirations of the human soul? That there is no possible realization back of these soulful endeavors?

Is Tantalus, after all, the creator and Father of Man? inspired only by love of disappointment, defeat, and despair, in his children?

*For one, I do not believe it.*

To plant these aspirations in the soul of man, and doom them to everlasting disappointment and defeat, would brand the creator of man as an Infinite Liar, instead of a Loving Father.

The earnest student must first learn to recognize, and to discriminate; for the "blind leaders of the blind" are always legions.

This power of discrimination, to which I have referred, goes deeper, and means far more, than most persons ever realize, and this is why so many are continually deceived.

It is the light of understanding, of spiritual intelligence, within the soul of man.

It may be likened to a traveler in a foreign country, and a strange land, suddenly hearing one speaking fluently his own language, his native tongue. It is impossible to deceive him. In this case, however, it is not the mere words, the inflection or pronunciation, but the ideas, sentiments, and principles expressed.

"Liberty, Fraternity, Equality," for example; or sympathy, Charity, and loving kindness.

The "sign of the Master" is at once recognized by one already prepared to receive and to understand it. The soul that really desires truth and wisdom above all things, has thereby developed the power to recognize it.

This is the discrimination referred to. It is not what someone else tells you, or what another claims. It is what *you* discern and recognize, and the teaching and the life are in perfect harmony, like chords in music; and they strike a harmonic chord in you, that may be first a surprise, and soon a great joy and a bright light.

It is not a question of authority, and of credentials, but of intrinsic reality. You must know how to assay and test the gold yourself. This is where the "Alchemy of the Great Work" comes in, and here lies the beginning of Adeptship, the preparation for the "Great Work." I can demonstrate this from a score of old books, some of them going back many centuries.

It has also been symbolized and picturegraphed 'til the imagination ran riot, and ingenuity and fancy became lost, like ideas in a fantasy of words.

I know of but one place, one Institution, in modern times, where these essential truths of the Great Work have been preserved as a consistent whole, and that is in the symbolism of Free Masonry, but the craft long ago lost the real interpretation, though many to-day are on the lines that lead to it.

The whole symbolism and ritual of the Blue Lodge in Masonry is, from beginning to end, *a symbol of the journey of the human soul on this earth*, from darkness to light; from sin to righteousness; from ignorance to wisdom and understanding.

In other words, it is an exact *theorem* and solution of the *Magnum Opus*; a symbol of the philosophy and accomplishment of the GREAT WORK.

The science and the theology of the present day have been briefly contrasted. Neither of them pretends to give us any real science of the human soul.

Science says frankly she "does not know." Theology bids us believe and obey; trust and hope. Philosophy speculates and reasons, while amusing itself with the kaleidoscope of "postulates" and "categories."

Science must deal with facts, demonstrate their actuality, and classify them; that is, find their natural order and sequence.

In psychology, the facts are *within* the realm of consciousness, and therefore their demonstration is a matter of individual experience. This is why psychology differs from all other sciences.

No one can transfer his individual experiences directly to another. He can describe how he gained them, and give the result and conclusions, and here is where those who know nothing of the real problem, are often both incredulous and contemptuous. The only answer to these is, "they are joined to their idols, let them alone." "They would not believe though one arose from the dead," and yet we are told again and again that the "School of Natural Science" is the "school of personal experience."

It may be well to reflect a moment, and ask ourselves, how it is that we really know anything? Is it not through personal experience? Real knowledge comes, and can come, in no other way.

No teacher of the real science of psychology can ever transmit or transfer his knowledge to another. All he can do is to describe the methods, and steps, by which he acquired it, and assist the student in acquiring it for himself in the same way, or under the same processes and laws.

We have only to reflect on the ordinary experiences of life, to realize that this is a universal principle and rule. In the deeper science of the soul, and the higher life, instead of this law being relaxed, it becomes all the more binding.

Do not the principles that adhere in atom, molecule and mass, still hold in worlds and solar systems? Is not this precisely what is meant by "The Reign of Law"? If man were built upon some other scheme or plan than the rest of nature, how could he apprehend or adjust himself to Nature? The very *concept* of miracle is *lawlessness*, and mystery is but another name for *ignorance*.

Knowledge means experience and apprehension of Law.

Neither can the laws of Nature and the laws of God be at cross-purposes, for that would make harmony impossible and inconceivable.

The confusion and discord are all in us, and the Great Work means adjustment, harmony, and then Knowledge.

It is the journey of the human soul on the Royal Highway to Light, Liberation, and Eternal Day.

For many centuries those who have achieved this Wisdom, this "Great Work," have been trying to make it accessible to mankind, and to place it in such form that the ethical, scientific, and philosophical principles involved, and upon which it is based, should not again be lost. Every such effort has hitherto failed.

The scientific spirit of the present age, in a very broad way, seemed to offer a new and a more advantageous opportunity; for the whole process is one of strict science.

The Psychology of the present day has become involved in phenomena and automatism, and is in no sense *constructive*. It is one thing to build theories, and quite a different thing to systematize demonstrated facts, through the recognition of co-ordinate relations, and underlying law.

The work is open and accessible to all who manifest real interest, an open mind, and who have the intelligence and discrimination to recognize the character of the work. It has never, in the history of man, been open in any other way, on any other terms, or to any other individuals.

Those who can fill these requirements constitute to-day a larger number than have before existed at any one time, for perhaps many centuries.

The "School of Natural Science" is in evidence. The "Great Work" is carefully outlined.

There is no bar to one's making a beginning on the path, except indifference, incredulity, preoccupation, or prejudice; and these need not be in the least disturbed, for they will be kindly and courteously passed by.

Arguments, controversy, and proselyting, have no part in the Great Work, as there is no organization, and no personal ambitions to serve.

Those who speak a common language, are inspired by a common purpose, and aspire to a common and universal good, will, soon or late, find themselves associated together and co-operating.

It is like a chorus of voices when an old song is started that we loved in childhood. Each takes up the strain, falls into his own part, and helps to swell the harmony, from the joy of his own heart.

Those who "never did like the song," will "quietly steal away." Both Swedenborg and Emerson have sufficiently illustrated the "Law of Correspondencies," and "compensation," to reveal the basis of all harmonious human associations, whether on the earth, or on other planes of being. Hence the "Harmonics of Evolution," was the forerunner of the "Great Work."

The pitiable byplay and claptrap of "Affinities" so often seen and heard nowadays, where all previous obligations are ignored, and personal responsibilities set at naught, only serve to emphasize the real law of harmony and constructive evolution, by showing what it is not.

The Great Work digs to the very foundations of life, and all human associations, and reveals the Good, the True, and the Beautiful, in the building of character, and the adornment of the Temple of the Human Soul.

This is indeed——

"Eternal Progress moving on,
From state to state the spirit walks."

Death is neither the end nor the beginning. It is only a change in pitch, a shifting of keys, and the same old Song of Life goes on, if we have but learned the score, and caught the harmony.

Salvation is not a thing accomplished once for all. We have only to consider the monotony, the poverty of invention, and imagination, of those who have tried to portray the joy of the Redeemed in heaven, in order to realize what a bore it would soon become, if that were all.

Inspiration, achievement, and eternal progress, with more and more helpfulness to others, with plane after plane achieved, revealing plane after plane beyond—does not this appeal far more strongly to the highest and best in us all?

And pray, what is this, but the *Great Work*, that I have tried herein to outline, and as taught and lived by Jesus, and every great Master the world has ever known? Each has achieved in his own degree, worded it in his own way, and "stepped out of sunlight into shade, to make more room for others."

Long before the birth of Jesus, it was said, "The wise and peaceful ones live, renewing the earth like the coming of Spring." And having themselves crossed the ocean of embodied existence, help all those who try to do the same thing, without personal motive.

I have endeavored to give a general outline of the Great Work, drawn from history, tradition, philosophy, and symbolism, down to the present year of grace. I find many corroborations, many things pointing in the same general direction. But I find but one concise and definite *formulation* of the *scientific theorem*, in which the outline is clear, and the analogy complete, and thereby made accessible and apprehensible to the open-minded and intelligent student.

Such students need experience no real difficulty in finding a clew to the labyrinth of life, or, as our ancient brothers put it in regard to the *Magnum Opus*—"a key to the closed palace of the king."

This is the purpose of the "Harmonic Series" of books. They need rest upon no authority beyond the intrinsic evidence of truth, on every page. If they are not consistent in themselves, then they must fall in pieces. The only appeal to the reader is: read them carefully, analyze your own mind and soul, and come to your own conclusions. If they find no response, no answering chord in you, then they were written for someone else, or in vain.

One further consideration remains to be noted at this time, as the question is sure to arise: "How about woman in the Great Work?" Seldom in the past has she received recognition, since the earliest days in Old India, though here and there have been the most noble women.

I heard Anna Dickinson, many years ago, open one of her famous lectures with these words, "I claim for man and woman alike, the right to attempt and win. I claim for man and woman alike, the right to attempt and fail."

It seems to me to-day, as it did more than thirty years ago, that this is the whole problem in a nutshell, and that any number of words could add nothing to the statement.

The Great Work is as open to woman as to man, and on the same terms. They have perhaps more to overcome in some directions, and  men more in others. This is like saying, "man and woman are different," that is all.

One thing is certain; there will never be an ideal social state on earth, or a heaven anywhere, except as men and women *co-operate* together for the happiness of each, and the highest, noblest, cleanest good of all, and this is only another phase or department of the Great Work.

# CHAPTER VII

## THE MODULUS OF NATURE AND THE THEOREM OF PSYCHOLOGY

The Science of Psychology, like any other science, must deal with demonstrated facts, classify them, and systematize the resulting categories.

Strictly logical conclusions drawn from categories of facts so derived, deserve the name of Science.

Science is, therefore, a definite method of arriving at exact conclusions. No other method can legitimately bear the name of science.

No one pretends to dispute the conclusions logically involved in the Binomial Theorem; or in the Parallelogram of forces; or in correlative mechanical equivalents; or in many of the known laws of chemistry and physiology.

When, however, we come to mental processes and psychical phenomena, the facts are so redundant, and so differently reported and apprehended, that argument, belief and prejudice, credulity and incredulity, overshadow and drown with a war of words all clear, scientific methods or conclusions.

But if man, as a whole, is a fact in nature; or if "God made Man a Living Soul," then the whole nature of man exists under law, and is apprehensible to science.

Man's function as a scientist is to read, to reflect, to weigh, to measure, and to understand.

There are those who object to Natural Science as applied to "Divine" things. They would preserve the mystery, and seem to prefer miracle and dogma to knowledge and law.

Their preference is to be respected, even though ignorance and superstition result. Since the domain of science, in America at least, is no longer restricted by ecclesiastic law, the conflict between Religion and Science has gradually disappeared, and the conflict is rather that between knowledge and ignorance, with ignorance on the wane.

"Things settled by long use, if not absolutely good, at least fit well together."

This transition period seems confusing to many earnest souls with its "New Thought," its "occultisms" and its "Lo here's" and "Lo there's." But through and beneath it all, may be heard a note of harmony, the promise and the potency of the triumph of light and knowledge.

We may not know the final results, but every sincere and earnest seeker may have the peaceful assurance that he is on the open highway that leads to the noblest and the best.

The assurance of knowledge but makes clearer the revelations of faith.

That "absentee God"—of which Carlyle wrote, has been discerned as the Universal Intelligence, and equally Love and Law.

Among recent writers and books on the subject of psychology, Professor Hugo Münsterberg's "Psychotherapy" occupies a very high place. It appeals especially to the physician, more familiar than others with morbid psychical states. Here I can look back on almost half a century of experience, the most active, in dealing with these cases.

But I am at present less concerned with mental pathology and therapy, than with the general psychological basis; the *causative* categories upon which they are based, and which occupy the first half of Münsterberg's book.

Dividing the whole subject—the content of consciousness, all the faculties, capacities and powers, all processes and sequences—into two general groups or classes, the *purposive* and the *causal*, Münsterberg declares that "the *causal* view only is the view of psychology"; "the *purposive* view lies outside of psychology."

I hold, that without the *purposive* view equally included and co-ordinated, there can be no such thing as Scientific Psychology. Half views will hardly admit of synthetic generalizations.

The complete separation here instituted, between the purposive and causal factors, in itself, for purposes of definition and study, need not be objected to, if it were consistently carried out, which it is not. He so nearly pre-empts the whole ground for the *causal*, giving scant courtesy to the *purposive*, merely a few crumbs of comfort, so that it cannot be said to be ignored altogether, and drops the scientific method entirely in dealing with it; assenting to moral precepts and principles, without a clew to any scientific basis, that one must object to the *name*—Psychology—as being applied to it at all. It contains no hint of a "knowledge of the Soul."

It is the Vito-Motor mechanism of the Mind. The Automatism of the elements, incidents, changes, and sequences of our states of consciousness; based upon, and including all that we know of physiology. Along these lines, Münsterberg's work has probably never been equaled. It is concise, comprehensive, and exhaustive.

His physical, physiological, and mental syntheses are well-nigh complete.

Whenever, in the future, what he calls "the *purposive* view" shall be resurrected from the obscurity and nescience to which he has assigned it, and really habilitated in the garb of Science, and recognized as the lawful spouse of the *causal*, we shall indeed have a true Psychology, a Science of the Human Soul.

Münsterberg neither scouts nor denies the possibility of such a future discovery. In the meantime, his viewpoint, and necessarily some of his conclusions and generalizations, are one-sided, and out of focus.

Emphasizing the *causal* as he does, this could hardly be otherwise; and from this point of view, and for this reason, his practical Psychotherapy is purely empirical.

We need not deny his facts, or his results, even when mixed with hypnosis, more than he does the "cures" in "Christian Science," "Faith Cures," at Lourdes, or by the "laying on of hands." All these things are too well known, and not one of them deserves the name of Science. They are solely empirical methods. Münsterberg's broader view and deeper analysis give to his methods great prominence, and he can point to no results that transcend the others. These facts and these results are as old as the history of man. They have, even as he points out, constituted epidemics of "cure."

There is, moreover, a scientific view and method regarding what he calls the purposive view which he overlooks entirely, and which by emphasis of the causal, makes seemingly impossible. It is our purpose to try and make this clear.

His analysis of Suggestion, though largely automatic, is well-nigh exhaustive. Awareness, and Attention, are illustrated copiously; but not clearly differentiated as they may be, and actually are in the experience of individual life.

Fortunately, and wisely, he eliminates the "Subconscious" as having no real meaning or scientific value as now used.

But it might be applied to the Mental awareness of physiological automatism (bodily habits, often beginning in an act of will, or attention; writing, speaking, music, dancing, and the like, and in less degree, all life impulses and movements below the line of attention or awareness).

If, by courtesy, these might be called sub-conscious, then there is another group above the habitual plane of awareness, that, by equal courtesy, might be called Supra-conscious. But, unless it is remembered, as Münsterberg points out, that, regardless of phenomena, *Consciousness is one*, these terms can only lead to confusion.

Certain cases designated "multiple" or "dissociated personalities" have only served to increase this confusion still further; and more especially, when the effort has been made to patch them together, or to control them from without, by hypnosis. The well-known case of "Sally," reported by Dr. Morton Prince, stands at last, as a "personally conducted" psychological excursion, with Sally still preserving her incognito, and as much a mystery as ever.

That automatism incident to all progressive organization and perfection of function, and through which physical, physiological, mental, and psychic synthesis becomes possible, has been allowed to usurp the place of the "Builder of the Temple," the "Driver of the Chariot," and the "Player" upon the "Harp of a thousand strings." Harmony and equilibrium are incidents resulting from *causative* processes! We need only to know the construction, relations of parts, and principles involved in the vibrations of the Harp, in order to understand and appreciate the music. The player, the musician—drunk, or sober, tone-blind or genius—is a mere incident, and however *purposive* or competent, is admitted by courtesy only, and warned not to interfere too much with the Harp!

To build, and keep in order, and tune the Harp, constitutes the science of music. Some day, when we have leisure and inclination, we may turn our attention to the Musician, but that day seems far off. We admit that his function is *purposive*. He, no doubt, has designs on the Harp, and upon us, but we are handling musical instruments at present, and if he objects to our calling ourselves "Musicians" (psychologists) he is impertinent, and should study the science of music, or keep silent.

I am not "begging the question" in regard to the human soul. I am simply emphasizing the fact of the Individual Intelligence, which, at the point of equilibrium, sweeps the strings with that harmony which is the soul of music.

This Harp of a thousand strings, is indeed, "fearfully and wonderfully made." Its physics and kinetics; its consonants and dissonants; its shifting keyboards; its changes in pitch, rhythm, and harmony from atom and molecule, to neurons, cells and mass; with the tides of life—blood, plasma, water, air, magnetism—sweeping the whole at every breath or pulse beat, to the cry of the builder—Life—"out with the old! in with the new!" and yet the *conscious identity* in health, typically unchanged and unchanging—*causative, designed, scientific*—yea verily! and *purposive, human, intelligent, spiritual, divine*, but a dead corpse, given over to decomposition the moment it is bereft of that something we feel, and know, and name—the *Individual Intelligence*—the Master Musician; or the staggering, drunk, crazy fiddler, with this Harp of a thousand strings, twanging perhaps in a mad-house!

Put the house in order; analyze, and classify; adjust the furniture with the handmaids of science, art, and beauty in evidence and at call; but for goodness' sake! stop hypnotizing the musician—"Just a little"—under the fallacy or the pretense of *strengthening* the Will by *weakening* it just a little more! This is "giving your patients fits, because you are death on fits"! Rescue Science from this atheromatous degeneration, and then suppress the dabblers in "black magic" who pose as Hypnotists, as Münsterberg advises.

For clear intelligence and exhaustive analysis, Münsterberg's "Psychotherapy" is a masterpiece, but his psychic equation of *causative* and *purposive*, with all his mathesis, not only remains unsolved, but leads to confusion, from the false light shed on the unknown quantity, and his failure to indicate the gnosis; the demarcation between automatism and purposive Intelligence.

That this confusion exists in the daily life of the average individual whose evolution is still incomplete; that it constitutes a large per cent. of all cases of "dominant ideas," obsessions, riotous emotions and passions; that it is nowhere recognized and defined in modern psychology, or made synthetically clear in modern philosophy, all these lapses make it all the more necessary that it should be clearly defined and made plain as the basis of Scientific Psychology.

In addition to all this, if Münsterberg's conclusions and applications are unsound because psychologically unscientific at the point; for example, where he almost hesitatingly indorses hypnosis, however qualified or safeguarded, he is certain to be quoted as authority on the subject by those who will ignore all his qualifications to justify the practice.

In order to meet these imperative conditions, the attempt to formulate any philosophy of psychology will not be made.

Even were such an attempt made successfully, that would remove the discussion from the field of science, where it should by all means remain. What we need is a real science of life, and this should involve the whole mental and psychical realm, and lead ultimately to a knowledge of the human soul.

Recognized facts in common experience only need be appealed to, though different values will have to be placed upon some of these facts as their importance is made plain.

We begin with the fact of consciousness. What it is, we do not know. What it means and does, we know very largely and broadly. In itself, it is purely passive. It never acts. Like space, it is the "all container." It is the background, the theatre of our intelligence.

With the individual intelligence, plus, or with consciousness, we have awareness. This is perception, or cognition, still negative.

These basic conditions, faculties and capacities, are like a company of soldiers on parade. Now comes the "word of command"—*Attention*!

Latent consciousness—awareness—now becomes concentrated, focalized on one point, one feeling, or emotion, or act. The soldiers "dress up," glance down the line, and are ready to act. Then comes the action, the movement, the drill, or the fight.

The drill master is also a soldier, but he is in command. He is called the Will. Without him and his recognized authority, the soldiers may be a mob, or a rabble. With him, they "fall in line," give "attention," "dress up," and are ready to act.

These are facts, and are basic and primary in our conscious *awareness* and *attention* in consciousness; the one negative, though inclusive; the other positive, and motor, or active.

In his "Psychotherapy" under the heading "The Subconscious," Münsterberg has much to say upon the meaning and differentiation of awareness, attention, and recognition, but he fails to point out in direct relation, at this point, the primary power—the Will, moved by the Individual Intelligence.

Later in his work the will is recognized and frequently referred to, but from beginning to end he makes it incidental, rather than basic. When he comes to broad groups of psychic phenomena, or pathological symptoms, the sounding board of Rational Volition is cracked and there is where hypnosis slips in.

Broad as he has laid his foundations in physical and physiological synthesis, he loses sight of its importance in the psychological; regarding as an incident that which is a basic principle of prime importance. Schopenhauer went, perhaps, as far to the opposite extreme. Perhaps "the truth will be found in the middle of the road."

The heir apparent, the prince regent, the lawful Sovereign, by heredity, by the laws of Nature, and "by the Will of God," in this Tabernacle of Man, is the Individual Intelligence; no matter whether we recognize or dispute his rightful authority. His Prime Minister is the Human Will; whether conspiring against, or co-operating with, the King. We may analyze the foundation of the kingdom, and the affairs of state, and designate them as *causative*, or *purposive*. We may see monarchy, or anarchy; democracy or republicanism; we may dethrone the king, and turn the state, literally, into a mad-house; but all the facts of nature, conscious awareness, and Scientific Psychology, cry, with one voice, Hail to the King! Long Live the King! I! Me! Mine! Myself! A fact so basic, that it is as patent to the child as to the man.

Now comes the Juggler, the little Joker. Münsterberg has sufficiently revealed the variety-stage, "the Subconscious," and his biography of the various individual players and troupes is very elaborate. They are, one and all, *Suggestions*. And suggestion is the "Juggler," and the "little Joker."

After the Intelligence and the Will, our awareness finds subjects and objects, ideas, images, pictures, percepts and concepts.

That all these, both within and without, are Suggestive; that one idea, or image, or object, suggests another, or others, no one will deny, who has ever *thought* about his own thinking. It is like saying, all mental pictures are composite; the elements of many kinds coming from many sources.

So far, *Suggestion* is all right. It is awareness of an idea, percept, concept, or act awakened, called to attention by another, with the question, how does it strike you? what do you think of it? what, if anything, do you wish, or propose to do about it?

It is purely negative, and suggests action or inhibition, without the slightest domination.

Remember that the Will—rational Volition—is that power, which, from the point of attention enables the individual to act, or refuse to consider, as he pleases.

If I suggest to my friend here in my library, that it is near train time; that he can go if he chooses or remain with me all night, he is free to act on the suggestion and go or stay as he chooses. I have called to his attention certain facts of time, place, or circumstance, but left his will untrammeled. If I am tired of him and wish him to go, or really wish him to stay, in either case it is still a suggestion, because I have left him free to act or not. But in this case certain tones of my voice, not direct by touching the will, but coloring the feelings or emotions, color both his preferences and my own. Even persuasion, the power of another example, the placing of certain views or considerations before another, all these but make the more clear and specific the suggestion. They reach the will through the inside, in the realm of ideation, and not from the outside, in the way of domination. All these things are essential elements in social intercourse.

If, however, I have a motive in wishing my friend to go, or to stay, and have determined in my own mind which it shall be; ignoring or overriding his own choice; and if I use my will, or passes, or touch his eyes, or forehead, with the purpose of concentrating *his* attention or will, on *my* wish, or idea, or command, it is no longer free choice with him, but domination; no longer suggestion, but hypnosis, pure and simple.

The confusion and juggling at this point has been made the sole excuse for hypnotism, through belittling or ignoring the importance, normal action, and supremacy of the human will.

No one denies that the exchange or forcible expression of ideas, percepts, mental pictures, or concepts, is suggestive. But the normal individual is free to accept or reject them.

Education, bias, prejudice, and the like, have also much to do in determining results.

But the moment you interfere with the free choice of the individual and dominate toward your choice, regardless of his own, you enter the realm of hypnosis; deprive him, just to that degree, of free choice, and might as well call it "fiddlesticks" as "suggestion." It is domination, the mastery, so far as it goes or exists at all, of the will, voluntary powers, and sensory organs of one individual, by the will of another; thus reversing completely the process of nature.

To dominate the will of another is to weaken it. Timidity, apprehension, fear, are in inverse ratio to confidence, self-assurance, courage, and self-control.

Health, happiness, and self-development lie along the lines of man's higher evolution, and the basic principle, the primary power, the minister of state, is the rational and intelligent Will.

The scientific theorem of Psychology can be nothing else than Nature's Modulus of Man, with its root in Universal Intelligence. Man individualizes and involves this Intelligence as he evolves form, function, adaptation, and adjustment, and at least secures and maintains perfect equilibrium.

This is Nature's Modulus, else the whole of human life is purposeless and meaningless.

Given, then, an Individual Intelligence, endowed with self-consciousness; with Rational Volition, the power to choose and to act or refuse to act; how shall it master its environment; adapt itself to any conditions; secure adjustment and become *Master*?

The starting point and the keynote from first to last is Self-Control.

Then come high Ideals, intelligent choice, and the will backed by discrimination and judgment. These lead to understanding and wisdom.

The "courage of one's convictions," can be neither conceited nor blatant egotism, but a readiness to assume full responsibility of motives, acts, and results.

This recognition of Personal Responsibility is what we call *Conscience*. It is the Judgment-seat of the Individual Intelligence in the Kingdom of its own Soul, or realm of consciousness. The moment this throne totters, or is obscured, devolution begins, and degeneration, insanity, and Inferno lie that way.

It does not change one principle involved, or weaken either Modulus or Theorem when we reflect that most equations are ended by death, long before being brought to successful solution. For the time they are certainly interrupted.

Neither do the babel of tongues, the theories, theologies, or philosophies change either Modulus or Theorem, because they are grounded in demonstrated facts, recognized, either vaguely or clearly, in the conscious experience of every intelligent thinking man and woman.

Constructive Psychology, based upon Science, for the building of character by persistent effort, increasing continually all personal resources, means the normal higher evolution of man.

So-called religions and the life after death have been purposely left unconsidered.

If we really have a Science of the Soul—the Individual Intelligence—based upon psychological facts, demonstrated in the daily experience of every healthy individual, it touches religion at its most vital point, viz.: ethics or morals. If these ethical principles are true and demonstrable, they must constitute the foundation of religion as of ethics. If morals are strengthened and made clear, and Personal Responsibility as Conscience, is recognized and accepted, the Vicarious Atonement will have to go, and Theologians will have to change their mystical and miraculous interpretations from Vicarious Atonement to personal at-one-ment with *Christos*.

The "miraculous conception," and "virgin birth," held equally in regard to Christna centuries before, and also the literal resurrection of the physical body will have to be otherwise explained.

The purposive view as one full term of the psychological equation, will find uniform law and order in place of the credulous legends of ignorant and superstitious monks, while the Divine Man will be taken down from the cross and restored to the heart of humanity, as the Modulus of Nature, *realized* as a normal evolution, under natural and spiritual law.

Salvation from sin, ignorance, superstition, and fear, will be recognized as the result of "Leading the Life," and Vicarious only through a divine example; or, if you please, *legitimate Suggestion*; with personal effort, rational volition, and personal responsibility working in harmony toward the desired result.

# SECTION TWO

# THE NEW AVATAR OF NATURAL SCIENCE

# CHAPTER VIII

## OUR INDEBTEDNESS TO ANCIENT INDIA

It is more than thirty years since in Southern Europe, England, and America, a genuine Renaissance of Vedic literature, philosophy, and religion began to assume a popular form and to become accessible to the general reading public.

Scholars, like Sir William Jones, had for the past century been familiar with the ancient civilization and the Vedic literature and the study of Sanscrit had made some progress in the Universities.

The idea, however, that these antiquities had any vital interest to us, beyond curious myths and obsolete superstitions, had not been perceived, much less admitted.

The antiquity of man, and the Philosophy of Evolution, had opened new fields for thought, and necessitated a revision of all previous concepts of man and nature.

Old records and interpretations were everywhere revised, and the interpretations of the Mosaic records were challenged at every point.

Popular religions were up in arms and were compelled to adjust themselves to the new régime.

But even after this century of progress and enlightenment, it has scarcely yet dawned on the mind of theologians that the challenge of science was, after all, insignificant, compared with that which was to come, and for which modern science had paved the way.

The whole realm of theology, and the foundations of religion, were to undergo revision.

Facts incontestable were being gathered and proofs established beyond all possible denial, or controversy, that all modern theologies and religions were copied and adapted from Vedic and ante-Vedic sources, antedating our present era by more than two thousand years.

The superficial and devout churchman, whose faith is fortified on the one hand by superstition, and on the other at least borders on fanaticism, is apt to be resentful in the presence of these facts, and, falling back on the infallibility and plenary inspiration of the Bible, to declare that if his own superficial interpretations are questioned or denied, Religion will be done for and mankind left in utter darkness.

He does not perceive that the facts of nature and the essentials of religion are one thing, and man's *interpretation* of them another thing entirely.

He does not perceive how these ignorant and superstitious interpretations of men have set at naught the real life of Jesus and the teachings of the Christ.

He does not realize how doctrine has usurped the place of duty, and dogmatism has hardened the soul of man.

One thing, however, is inevitable. Facts and evidence as to origin, analogies, and adaptation of the Christian Mysteries from ancient India, are widely known, and the time has come when these mysteries are being examined as to their intrinsic meaning and their bearing on the daily life of man and the progress of the human race.

The author of this little book has only attempted a bare outline of these great facts, and to put them in such shape that the reader may perceive their general bearing, and the sources whence they are derived.

The following extracts made almost at random, the quantity of evidence being so redundant, from Jacolliot's "Bible in India," a translation of which was made in this country as early as **1873**, and Prof. Max Müller's Lectures, "India, What Can It Teach Us?" printed here more than a quarter of a century ago, will give the reader the evidence and the assurance that these ancient sources of wisdom are scarcely yet known in outline to the Western World.

Jacolliot spent many years in India, studying its present civilization and its ancient lore, while Prof. Max Müller derived his knowledge largely from study of Sanscrit and the Vedanta.

"Soil of Ancient India, cradle of humanity, hail! Hail, venerable and efficient nurse, whom centuries of brutal invasion have not yet buried under the dust of oblivion! Hail, fatherland of faith, of love, of poetry, and of science. May we hail a revival of thy past in our Western future.

"I have dwelt 'midst the depths of your mysterious forests, seeking to comprehend the language of your lofty nature, and the evening airs that murmured 'midst the foliage of banyans and tamarinds whispered to my spirit these three magic words: Zeus, Jehovah, Brahma.

"I have inquired of Brahmins and priests under the porches of temples and ancient pagodas, and they have replied:

"'To live is to think, and to think is to study God, who is all, and in all....

"'To live is to learn, to learn is to examine and to fathom in all their perceptible forms the innumerable manifestations of celestial power.

"'To live is to be useful; to live is to be just; and we learn to be useful and just in studying this book of the Vedas, which is the word of eternal wisdom, the principle of principles as revealed to our fathers.'"

Plotinus, the Neoplatonist, said: "God is not the principal of beings, but the principle of principles."

This was the Hindoo concept of *Para Brahm* two thousand years before.

"In the whole world there is no study so beneficial and so elevating as that of the Upanishads. It has been the solace of my life—it will be the solace of my death. [Schopenhauer, quoted by Max Müller.] ... If I were to look over the whole world to find out the country most richly endowed with all the wealth, power and beauty that nature can bestow—in some parts a very paradise on earth—I should point to India. If I were asked under what sky the human mind had most fully developed some of its choicest gifts, has most deeply pondered on the greatest problems of life, and has found solutions of some of them which well deserve the attention even of those who have studied Plato and Kant—I should point to India. And if I were to ask myself from what literature we, here in Europe, we who have been nurtured almost exclusively on the thoughts of Greeks and Romans, and of one Semitic race, the Jewish, may draw that corrective which is most wanted in order to make our inner life more perfect, more comprehensive, more universal, in fact more truly human, a life, not for this life only, but a transfigured and eternal life—again I should point to India."

The reader should remember that this is not the *opinion* of an ignorant enthusiast, but the mature judgment of one of the most profound scholars and Sanscritists in Europe in his day—Prof. Max Müller.

"The study of Mythology has assumed an entirely new character, chiefly owing to the light that has been thrown on it by the ancient Vedic Mythology of India.

"Buddhism is now known to have been the principal source of our legends and parables."

The story of the two women who claimed each to be the mother of the same child is found literally in the Kanjur, translated from the Buddhist Tripitake, and the "Judgment of Solomon" is only a copy of the older story.

"The history of all histories, and yet the mystery of all mysteries—take religion, and where can you study its true origin, its natural growth and its inevitable decay better than in India, the home of Brahmanism, the birthplace of Buddhism, and the refuge of Zoroastrianism.

"Take any of the burning questions of the day—popular education, higher education, parliamentary representation, codification of laws, finance, emigration, poor-law, and whether you have anything to teach and to try, or anything to observe and to learn, India will supply you with a laboratory such as exists nowhere else.

"And in the study of the history of the human mind, and the study of ourselves, of our true selves, India occupies a place second to no other country. Whatever sphere of the human mind you may select for your special study, whether it be language, or religion, or mythology, or philosophy, whether it be laws or customs, primitive art or primitive science, everywhere, you have to go to India, whether you like it or not, because some of the most valuable and most instructive materials in the history of man are treasured up in India, and in India only.

"Sleeman tells us men (in India) adhere habitually and religiously to the truth, and 'I have had before me hundreds of cases,' he says, 'in which a man's property, liberty, and life have depended upon his telling a lie, and he has refused to tell it.' Could many an English judge say the same?" (Remarks by Prof. Müller.)

Prof. Müller quotes from an Arabian writer of the thirteenth century, "The Indians are innumerable, like grains of sand, free from all deceit and violence. They fear neither death nor life."

And again, from Marco Polo, in the thirteenth century, "You must know, Marco Polo says, that these Abralaman (Hindoos) are the best merchants in the world, and the most truthful, for they would not tell a lie for anything on earth."

"In the sixteenth century Abu Fazl, the minister of the Emperor Akbar, says in his 'Ayin Akbari,' 'The Hindus are religious, affable, cheerful, lovers of justice, given to retirement, able in business, admirers of truth, grateful and of unbounded fidelity, and their soldiers know not what it is to fly from the field of battle.'"

(How badly these "poor heathen" were in need of the Jesuit missionary, and the British government and civilization!)

Prof. Müller quotes Warren Hastings regarding the Hindus in general, as follows, "They are gentle and benevolent, more susceptible of gratitude for kindness shown them, and less prompted to vengeance for wrongs inflicted, than any people on the face of the earth—faithful, affectionate, submissive to legal authority."

Bishop Heber said, "The Hindus are brave, courteous, intelligent, most eager for knowledge and improvement, sober, industrious, dutiful to parents, affectionate to their children, uniformly gentle and patient, and more easily affected by kindness and attention to their wants and feelings than any people I ever met with."

Elphinstone said, "No set of people among the Hindus are so depraved as the dregs of our own great towns." (It might have been wiser to have employed English missionaries at home.)

Sir Thomas Munro bears even stronger testimony. He writes, "If a good system of agriculture, unrivaled manufacturing-skill, a capacity to produce whatever can contribute to either convenience or luxury, schools established in every village for teaching reading, writing and arithmetic, the general practice of hospitality, and charity among each other, and above all, a treatment of the female sex full of confidence, respect, and delicacy, are among the signs which denote a civilized people—then the Hindus are not inferior to the nations of Europe—and if civilization is to become an article of trade between

England and India, *I am convinced that England will gain by the import cargo.*

"Even at the present moment, after a century of English rule and English teaching, I believe that Sanskrit is more widely understood in India, than Latin was in Europe at the time of Dante.

"There are thousands of Brahmans, even now, when so little inducement exists for Vedic studies, who know the whole of the Rig-Veda by heart, and can repeat it, and what applies to the Rig-Veda, applies to many other books." (Ten thousand and seventeen hymns.)

Speaking of other and later literature, Prof. Müller says, "It is different with the ancient literature of India, the literature dominated by the Vedic and Buddhistic religions. That literature opens to us a chapter in what has been called the Education OF THE HUMAN RACE, TO WHICH WE CAN FIND NO PARALLEL anywhere else. Whoever cares for the historical growth of our language, that is, of our thoughts; whoever cares for the intelligible development of religion and mythology, whoever cares for the first foundation of what in later times we call the sciences of astronomy, metronomy, grammar and etymology; whoever cares for the first intimations of philosophical thought; for the first attempts at regulating family life, village life, and state life, as founded on religion, ceremonial, tradition and contact (Samaya), must in future pay the same attention to the literature of the Vedic period as to the literature of Greece and Rome and Germany.

"I maintain then that for a study of man, or, if you like, for a study of Aryan humanity, there is nothing in the world equal in importance with the Veda.

"The aristocracy of those who know—*di color che sanno*—or try to know, is open to all who are willing to enter, to all who have a feeling for the past; an interest in the genealogy of our thoughts, and a reverence for the ancestry of our intellect, who are, in fact, historians in the true sense of the word, i.e. inquirers into that which is past, but not lost.

"But if we mean by primitive the people who have been the first of the Aryan race to leave behind literary relics of their existence on earth, then I say the Vedic poets are primitive; the Vedic language is primitive; the Vedic religion is primitive, and, taken as a whole, *more primitive than anything else that we are ever likely to recover in the whole history of our race....*

"For this reason, because the religion of the Veda was so completely guarded from all strange infection, it is full of lessons which the student of religion could learn nowhere else."

The foregoing quotations have been made from a little volume, "India: What Can It Teach Us?" published by Funk and Wagnalls in **1883**, and sold at **25** cents, so that these statements of Prof. Max Müller have been accessible for more than a quarter of a century.

Since **1883**, however, we have heard more and more of the "Wisdom of Old India."

The whole Theosophical movement, degenerate as it may have become in some directions, and much as it has been misinterpreted, and ridiculed and exploited in others, was primarily a sincere and earnest attempt "to bring the Secret Doctrine of ancient India within reach of Western students," to promote the brotherhood of man; the study of ancient philosophy and the psychical powers latent in man.

121

There are thousands of intelligent and earnest students all over the world who have been uplifted, illuminated, and encouraged by these studies. When the true history of the present epoch comes to be written, there can be no shadow of doubt as to the recognition that will be accorded to H. P. Blavatsky and her aims, her life, and her work.

But such movements as are going on in the world, continually change their base, their methods, and their prospective. While the new awakening unmistakably goes back to old India, and compels a review and a readjustment of all our knowledge, and all our hopes and aims, another spirit has entered our intellectual realm, and compelled attention and recognition.

It has made for itself a habitation and a name, and nothing less than a cataclysm can altogether overthrow it.

It is the Genius of Scientific Criticism, Research, and Demonstration.

The "Mistakes of Moses" may indeed be paralleled by those of modern physical science, and these are being revealed side by side with those of theology and dogmatic assertion.

It has hardly yet dawned upon the mind of the physical scientist that the concept of the psychical and spiritual life and nature of man comprises, with the world of matter and form, a complete theorem of human life. He is often as incredulous, resentful, and contemptuous as the creed-bound religionist at the approach of more light, and the suggestion that all these essential problems were included and solved ages ago in ancient Aryavarta; and that "the few who know," the ancient order of the *Illuminati*, now designated the "School of Natural Science," has treasured this knowledge for ages.

The Vedas are not only ancient, but complicated and diffuse, and the busy life of the modern student will hardly suffice for the mastery of their wisdom, or the understanding of their secrets.

When, however, this ancient wisdom is condensed and epitomized, in perfect harmony with the concepts, the methods, and the demonstrations of Natural Science, the "Jewel in the Lotus,"—to use a Vedic synonym,—will appear in all its beauty and glory, to all who have eyes to see, and ears to hear, with determination to "honor every truth by use," and loyal service.

In the foregoing quotations it may be seen what this real knowledge did for the people of ancient India in building character on constructive lines, promoting justice, equity, charity, and kindness among the common people, and the teeming millions of India, when our Saxon and Norman ancestors were still barbarians, and before the Jew or the Christian were even dreamed of.

In the following quotations from Jacolliot's "Bible in India," an outline will be given as to the source of some of our myths, pantheons, and religions.

These brief and imperfect outlines from two small and generally forgotten books, ought to satisfy any intelligent and unbiased student how completely the general thesis may be demonstrated from the ancient records themselves.

The books from which these quotations are made are like kindergarten primers for the use of beginners.

The present writer's interest in and study of Theosophy and the Secret Doctrine were instigated by Schopenhauer's "World as Will and Idea." He found how largely Schopenhauer had drawn from the Upanishads (see previous quotation), and how little, after all, his "Philosophy" had utilized the ancient Wisdom. Hence he resolved to seek the ancient sources of knowledge, and has been trying his best to apprehend and utilize them, the hoarded wisdom of the ages.

He is not in the least anxious to gain recognition for, or to seek to rehabilitate old India, for its own sake. She speaks for herself, through the centuries of the past, and will continue to speak and to influence all coming time.

Jacolliot shows, however, a little irritation at this point over the suppression of facts, the brutality of marauding invaders, and the wholesale and brazen appropriation without the least credit to India's store of wisdom.

The present writer is, however, exceedingly desirous that his fellow-students in the West should discover, recognize, and utilize this ancient mine of wisdom for themselves.

Its day of recognition is just now at the dawn, and the most pressing problems concerning the real nature, the spiritual possibilities, and the eternal destiny of the soul of man, are pressing and burning questions to-day.

That these problems do not wait solution by modern physical science and physio-psychology, but await only the understanding and acceptance of every earnest and intelligent student, is easily demonstrated. It challenges the world to-day, as it has not done before for many millenniums, and the issues are to be tried out to a scientific demonstration.

The preferences and prejudices of partisans will not be consulted, nor will they in the least interrupt the progress, nor interfere with the solution.

The question is no longer, "What think ye of Jesus?" but "What *know* ye of your own soul?" A new faith will supersede the old superstitions.

Faith, from the viewpoint of Natural Science, is "the soul's intuitive *conviction* of that which both reason and conscience approve." Blind faith, or belief, is ever the handmaid of superstition. The new faith is the harbinger, the promise, and the potency of knowledge, the anchor of the soul, and the armor of righteousness.

This is indeed the language of confidence, and it should be put to the test of science and experience.

The scornful and the contemptuous are not even *invited*! They are left alone with their Idols.

Coming now more directly to the splendid work of Jacolliot, one thing I think ought to be apparent to every honest and intelligent reader of "The Bible in India," and that is, that its author is in no sense a partisan of Hinduism, but a searcher and witness for the simple Truth as he finds and apprehends it.

He puts aside mystery, miracle, and Divine Revelation, as dispassionately in the Vedic, Brahmanical, and Buddhistic cults, as in the Mosaic and Christian. Belief in God, and reverence for Truth in the light of reason and conscience, shine from every page of his work.

To flippantly call him an "atheist," or a "destroyer of holy things," as though that were in any sense an answer to his thesis, and which formerly was the rule, and may even now be attempted in certain quarters, will simply brand the bigot as by no means intelligent—if indeed honest—who attempts it. The majority of such sectarians have grown wise or prudent enough to ignore all such issues.

There has been a great change in public sentiment since Jacolliot went to India as an earnest student of these subjects, and in the nearly forty years since he wrote this book.

The saying that "Truth passes through three phases before being accepted," specially applies here. First, people say, "It is not true." Second, "It contradicts Scripture," and when it at last is triumphant, that *"Everybody knew it before."*

The truths of which Jacolliot writes have already reached at least the beginning of the third stage. Of course, "Everybody" here means those who read, and think, and dare to use conscience and reason.

In referring to a religious debate between a missionary and a Brahman, and the universal interest manifested among all classes as to the outcome of the encounter, "hooting the vanquished in either case with strict impartiality," Jacolliot adds, "We shall be less surprised at this when it is known that there is not a Hindoo, whatever his rank or caste, who does not know the principles of the Holy Scripture, that is, the Vedas, and who does not *perfectly know how to read and write.*"

Three hundred and forty millions of people, thousands of them pariahs and outcasts, sharing refuse with the dogs, with no rights that any one else is bound to respect, bowing their faces in the dust when a Brahman passes ten paces away—and yet everyone can read and write!

Max Müller said he had had in his study at Oxford a young Hindoo who could repeat the whole of the Mahabharata *without missing a word or an inflection* from beginning to end.

These are some of the *remnants* in the decline of old India after thousands of years of Brahman rule and slavish domination of the people to preserve their own exclusive caste and exploitation. Western people have yet to learn the inevitable tendency, and the invariable rule of exploitation of the people, by a dominant priesthood, and the poverty and degradation of the masses that always results. It has never once failed in this result in three thousand years.

The whole of Southern Europe is already awakening to a realization of this result to-day. It is accomplished in the name of "Religion" by those who call themselves "Viceregents of God," and who arrogantly trample on the rights of conscience, and the freedom of man.

Brahmanism first set the example as originators of this slavish abomination.

The studies and investigations of Jacolliot in India, go back to the Vedic or pre-Brahmanic age; then to the rise, development, and slow decline of Brahmanism; then the epoch of Christna; the influence of Buddha, and his being driven out of India by the powerful Brahmans; and finally, to the present poverty and degradation of the millions through foreign invasion and domination.

The ruling Brahmans had neither thought nor desire for *Constructive Nationality*. In their pride and lust for power and gold, even in their just pride over their inheritance from Vedic ancestors, and wisdom, Patriotism was unknown to them. Invaders contended with them in robbing and enslaving the people.

The people who despised and hated the foreign invader dare not, even yet, to rise against their real despoilers—the Brahmans—or defy or break their power.

It is the Vedic literature, and the earliest, or pre-Brahmanic time that Jacolliot lauds so highly, and in which he finds and demonstrates, the existence of the sources of all human knowledge.

It will be ignorant folly, therefore, for the bigot and the sectarian to attempt to answer or oppose him, by referring to the condition of the people of India as it is to-day.

Jacolliot simply shows the causes that have led to the present degradation.

It is *priestcraft*, despite the Vedic wisdom, and the missions and teaching of Christna and Buddha.

All this Jacolliot demonstrates beyond all controversy.

The bulk of his work consists in demonstrating the source of Greek and Roman Mythology, Language, Law, Philosophy, etc., and equally of every Jewish and Christian doctrine and tradition.

Jacolliot shows that as the French code is copied or adapted from the Justinian, so equally the Justinian was derived from that of Manu, many centuries previously. And what is true of Law is equally true of philosophy, theology, morals, and the principles of science, art, architecture, and all the rest.

The Hindoos were demoralized by the priests, but the moral degradation extended even to them, and the arms they employed were turned against themselves.

"The first result of the baneful domination of priests in India was the abasement and moral degradation of woman, so respected and honored during the Vedic period.

"If you would reign over the persons of slaves, over brutalized intelligence, the history of these infamous epochs presents a means of unequaled simplicity. *Degrade and demoralize the woman*, and you will soon have made of man a debased creature, without energy to struggle against the darkest despotisms; for, according to the fine expression of the Vedas, 'the woman is the soul of humanity.'"

As did the Brahman priesthood, when through greed and ambition they forsook the ancient wisdom, so do the priesthood of Rome, with their celibacy added to the abominations and opportunities of the confessional.

Search the records of all time, and the traditions and customs of every people, and you will find nowhere else such recognition and reverence paid to woman as in the early Vedic days.

"Let it be well understood," says Jacolliot, "that it was but sacerdotal influence and Brahminical decay that, in changing the primitive condition of the East, reduced woman to a state of subordination which has not yet disappeared from our social system.

"Let us read these maxims taken at hazard from the sacred books of India." (I quote only a few.) "Man is strength—woman is beauty; he is the reason that governs, but she is the wisdom that moderates; the one cannot exist without the other, and hence the Lord created them two, for the one purpose.

"He who despises woman, despises his mother.

"Who is cursed by a woman, is cursed by God.

"The tears of woman call down the fire of heaven on those who make them flow.

"The songs of women are sweet in the ears of the Lord; men should not, if they wish to be heard, sing the praise of God without women.

"Women should be protected with tenderness, and gratified with gifts, by all who wish for length of days.

"It was at the prayer of a woman that the Creator pardoned man; cursed be he who forgets it." (See the Vedic "Garden of Eden.")

Moses, trained only in the decay of the old religion by the degenerate priests of Egypt, while drawing his legend of creation from the ancient Vedic source, reverses all this and places the blame of the "Fall" on woman, and the women of the Bible are more often concubines and prostitutes than Love's pure evangels as in the ancient days. Jacolliot proves this from many citations, as witness also the following: (Numbers, Chapter XXI.)

"And Moses was enraged against the chief officers of the army, against the tribunes, and the centurions who returned from battle.

"And he said unto them, Why have you saved the women and the children?

"Slay therefore all the males amongst the children, and the women who have been married.

"But reserve for yourselves all the young girls who are still virgins."

Moses spoke "in the name of God," as does his Holiness at Rome to-day. Comment is hardly necessary. A few more quotations from the Vedas:

"A virtuous woman needs no purification, for she is never defiled, even by contact with impurity.

"Women should be shielded by fostering solicitude by their fathers, their brothers, their husbands, and the brothers of their husbands, if they hope for great prosperity.

"When women are honored, the divinities are content, but where they are not honored, all undertakings fail."

The sacerdotal caste in Egypt followed the inspiration of the Brahmans, and took care to make no change in that situation.

And Moses followed the example of the priests of Egypt, where woman was a slave or a prostitute in the temples as out.

The degeneracy of a people, the decay of religion, and the degradation of woman are inseparable, and it is so-called "religion" that institutes the change, and sets the pace, "down the steep descent."

The Brahmans "forgot God" and instituted the worship of saints and holy men, and mythological characters, just as Rome does to-day. The women of America to-day by a consensus of public opinion should make auricular confession *disreputable*.

Excommunication, which is such a power in the hands of Rome, is merely a subterfuge and substitute for the degradation of "outcasts," and pariahs, instituted by the Brahman priests to terrify the disobedient and retain their power.

If the reader cares to know the danger and the degradation to woman fostered and protected through the Confessional by the Celibate Roman priesthood, he should read "The History of Auricular Confession," by De Lasteyrie, translated into English and printed in London in . Now and then a Pope or a council undertook to institute reform, but found, as in Spain, prostitution of women by priests through the confessional so widespread and universal that they more often gave up the attempt through fear of scandal and contempt for the Church itself.

Lecky, in his "History of European Morals," records the case of "the abbot-elect of St. Augustine, at Canterbury, who in **1171** was found on investigation to have *seventeen illegitimate children in a single village*; or, an abbot of St. Pelayo, in Spain, who in was proved to have kept no less than seventy concubines; or Henry III, Bishop of Liège, who was deposed in for having sixty-five illegitimate children."

132

If the reader remarks that "this is ancient history," he should remember that a celibate priesthood to-day have the same opportunity, through the secrecy and power of the Confessional, as ever.

I have barely touched on this disgusting but all-important question on the general thesis of Jacolliot, viz.: "The first result of the baneful domination of priests in India was the abasement and moral degradation of woman."

Rome, who derived her religious code from paganized Egypt, added celibacy to the opportunities and inducements for the degradation of woman. Rome never attained the heights from which the Brahman priesthood plunged into debauchery. Even to-day in the festivals in the Brahman temples wholesale orgies of prostitution are sometimes found, as witnessed and recorded by Jacolliot. From the first, Brahman priests have married and reared families. Their degradation and debauchery, therefore, cannot be charged to their original "Divine Revelation," but to their corruption of it.

I have given a few brief quotations among hundreds recorded by Jacolliot as to the respect and veneration accorded to woman in early Vedic times, and in the Laws of Manu.

"The Brahman may not approach the altar of sacrifice *but with a soul pure, in a body undefiled.*

"Spirituous liquors beget drunkenness, neglect of duty, and they profane prayer.

"The antiquity of India stands forth to establish its priority of religious legislation in prohibiting to priests the use of spirituous liquors, and especially in forbidding the pleasures of love when they are about to offer sacrifice.

"The woman whose words and thoughts and person are pure is a celestial balm.

"Happy shall he be whose choice is approved by all the good.

"It is ordained that a devotee shall choose a wife from his own class.

"The Brahman who marries a woman who is not a virgin, who is a widow, or divorced by her husband, or who is not known as a virtuous woman, cannot be permitted to offer sacrifice, for he is impure, and nothing can cleanse him from his impurities."

And Jacolliot adds, "It is not recorded, says the divine Manu, that a Brahman has ever, even by compulsion, married a girl of low class.

"Let the Brahman espouse a Brahmine, says the Veda.

"Let him take a well-formed virgin, of an agreeable name, of the graceful carriage of the swan, or of the young elephant, whose body is covered with light down, her hair fine, her teeth small, and her limbs charmingly graceful."

Jacolliot compares these early Vedic injunctions with Leviticus, Chapter XXI, and the absurdities introduced by Moses as to a "crooked nose or a squint eye."

Woman here in the West is just emerging from the slavery and degradation of ages, and she *ought* to know that that degradation was not the handicap of barbaric and undeveloped races, so far as the Aryan race is concerned, but a demoralization and degradation instituted by priests, in the name of religion, through which they have sought to rule the world, and so far as institutional religions are concerned, woman has had to progress *in spite of them.*

Without the aid and influence of woman to-day, neither Protestant nor Roman Church could exist at all, as witness almost any Sabbath service where women outnumber men often ten to one.

One day woman will be wise enough and brave enough to dictate terms, as she did ages ago in old Aryavarta. When that day comes, and the really Divine Motherhood planted in every true woman's soul is recognized by man and woman alike, God grant that she may thenceforth hold the fort till the Kali-Yuga is at full tide, and the Spiritual Evolution of our present Humanity is fully accomplished.

In the meantime the world will have learned to *know* Jesus, who and what he was, and how he became the Christ, and will have joined in his Divine Mission to man, as the teeming millions joined in old India under Christna ages ago.

# CHAPTER IX

## HERO WORSHIP AND FOLKLORE

The history of every people, of all time, and of every religion of which we have any record, reveals a similar origin, course, and destiny.

We of the present day have the advantage of these records upon which to institute comparisons, ascertain relations, and draw conclusions.

True, the partisans and postulants of all these religions at the present day will claim exception in favor of their own cult, and regard as sacrilegious and profane any attempt to institute comparisons and draw general conclusions.

Any attempt to persuade them of their error would be useless.

The essentials of their religion will not be called in question, but on the other hand, they will find that it is impossible to escape from the habitual and universal tendencies in which they are involved.

However veritable may have been the original revelations, the tendencies and habits of weaving around them the traditions and superstitions of folklore seem to have been inevitable and universal.

It is the province of Science to ascertain the facts in any given case, to institute comparisons, and to draw deductions and generalizations dispassionately and relentlessly.

It is thus that every tradition, superstition, creed, dogma, and revelation comes under review, and is placed on trial.

True science has no preconceived notion, no foregone conclusion. Each subject examined must tell its own story and in its own way, and stand or fall measured by intrinsic evidence and revealed fact.

To this tribunal every episode in the life of man and the history of the human race must at last come.

What are the *facts*? What do they reveal and signify?

To most religionists this method and aim of science seem as relentless and dogmatic as their own creed or dogmas.

It is a sifting and discriminative process, that, while relentless, is in the end eminently Just, and in the end will be found to be the revealer of all that is essential and true in religion itself.

In itself, science is not and never can be a religion.

It is a *method* only, which, like a search-light, reveals all religions in all their essentials, and places them in their true light.

Religion *per se* is an essential element in the nature and life of man and of the human race.

Science is a method, a way of procedure in the intelligent mind of man in its search for truth.

Religion is vital, essential, basic. It is born of the relation which inheres in the kinship of the individual intelligence to the Universal Spirit of Nature and of all life.

Science is the intelligent and rational use of the mental powers of man.

Religion is intuitional, spiritual perception, involving the heart, the affections. Man aspires, worships, adores, and by the light of Faith or intuitive conviction, recognizes that which he cannot explain and cannot get rid of if he tries.

Science is the just weight and measure of things seen, and of the natural causes of phenomena.

Religion—the evidence of things unseen. Religion, as a *fact*, can never be explained away by Science.

The so-called science that assumes or undertakes to do that, is materialism and nescience.

Superstition is the false interpretation of religion, and folklore and tradition are the accretions that gather around the foundations and original revelations of religion, and lead at last to obscuration and the need of a new revelation.

Each genuine new "revelation" is but the rehabilitation of the primeval religion in which accretions, false interpretations, and dogmatic assertions are cast aside.

Religion represents man's endeavor to apprehend and interpret the unseen; that "something more" and "something beyond" the visible, the sensuous, and the tangible.

It is this conscious *awareness* of something more and something beyond the visible and the tangible, that furnishes man with a conception of God and of the human soul. This is a natural intuition, inseparable from the *awareness* of self. It lies at the foundation like man's self-conscious identity, and can neither be explained nor explained away.

Here lies the root of all religions. The imagery of man's imagination, in his effort to apprehend the unseen, and to formulate the unknown, gives rise to myths, allegory, tradition, folklore, and in the end, to superstition, creed, and dogma.

Then come priestcraft, oppression, persecution. The death of religion, the deification of the revealer or *Avatar*, and the substitution of the priesthood as of divine authority, in place of the *revealer* or the revelation.

Jove, Orpheus, Jehovah, and at last Jesus, are enthroned beyond the clouds, and priest or church assume the earthly prerogative, speak in their place, assume dogmatic authority, promise heaven and happiness for obedience, and dire penalties for disobedience, and resort to persecution to maintain their authority.

The traditions, mythologies, and folklore of all the past have thus arisen. The creeds and dogmas of the present constitute the effort of man to assume exclusive dominion, and to exercise divine authority over the masses of mankind. It is only another form of the ambition of individuals for wealth, fame or power, lifting them to a "class" above the toiling, suffering, and sorrowing masses.

There are exceptional individuals all along the way, who conceive, hold, and exercise the spirit of the Master, and sink self in the service of man, and  but for these the organized priesthood would be execrated by mankind long before.

The organized church deifies, where the true disciple humanizes and helps mankind in the name and in the spirit of the Master.

This is the spirit, the origin, the genius and the history of every Avatar, of Christna, and all the Buddhas, the Saviors and Redeemers of history.

The orthodox Christian of to-day, whether Catholic or Protestant, will be likely to admit the foregoing outline except as it applies to his own religion. Whereas it is abundantly proven to-day regarding his own religion as nowhere else in history.

The histories of former religions are vague, distant, and so covered over by tradition, myth, and folklore, as to be difficult to trace.

The beginnings, history, and progress of the Christian religion are comparatively nearer at hand, and the process above outlined readily demonstrable.

Not only so, but the recognition of the facts and processes is everywhere in evidence.

This fact, however, by no means ends the controversy.

Traditions, creeds, and dogmas die hard, and fight to the last extremity. Nothing else known to man fights so desperately and dies so hard as an organized priesthood, and beyond this, they are upheld by the ignorance, superstition, the fear, and the faith of the masses.

Their adherents often believe and assume that they have discovered final truths, essential and unalterable verities.

They undertake to support and to maintain these by dogmatic authority, a holy book, a "thus sayeth the Lord."

"There it is, down in black and white." No further evidence is required.

To question such authority is to be damned. To believe, accept, and to conform, is to be *saved*.

Difference of opinion and of interpretation inevitably arise, even among those who dare not question the ultimate authority and genuineness of the original revelation. Hence arise sects, schisms, and theological warfare.

Notwithstanding all this, the original revelation becomes a matter of thorough investigation and of criticism.

The so-called "higher criticism" had already discovered errors in translation, and contradictions in interpretation, resulting in a "revised edition" of the sacred books, while under the name "*Pragmatism*," certain metaphysical writers and accredited teachers have undertaken to determine essential meanings and interpretations, and to submit religious revelations, creeds, dogmas, and theologies to critical analysis.

How far this analysis has gone, and how little of the original interpretation actually remains, only they are aware who keep abreast of current thought, and who with open mind care more for the simple truth than for custom, tradition, theologies, and the folklore of the past.

Dogmatic theological authority is completely undermined, and its days are numbered.

With the masses there is the habitual unrest, the feeling of uncertainty, the social upheaval, with the inevitable tendency to confusion and anarchy. A new religion is already in the formative stage, a new Avatar inevitable.

It is to be less a repudiation than a revision and rehabilitation of the old religion.

People everywhere are looking for the new revelation, for the coming of *Christos*, for the new Avatar, and few are aware that he is already here.

It should be borne strictly in mind that in every instance in the past, the advent of the Avatar has been unattended by signs and wonders, has come upon the stage of human action in the most commonplace way, and that myth, miracle, and folklore have followed as time went on.

To the people of his time Jesus was the "son of the carpenter," whose family was obscure. He came "eating with publicans and sinners."

Jesus, the demigod of to-day, was unknown and undreamed of in Galilee. Philo Judæus seems never to have heard of him.

What and who Jesus was, and what he did, is separated from what the church and theologians have made of him by a gulf that seems almost impassable, and yet this gulf has already been bridged and passed.

The new Avatar has for its mission the rehabilitation of Jesus as he actually existed, divested of all myth and miracle, while the mission for which he came, and the doctrines for which he lived and died are to be completely restored to mankind in their purity.

The old Hindoos would call this transformation a "reincarnation of Vishnu," a "new Avatar."

It will mean Jesus the divine Man, the master, *Christos*, restored to the heart of Humanity from the mysticism and miracle of monks and theologies, from the superstitions and folklore of the multitude.

This means a reconstruction and a restatement of the religion of Jesus.

Jesus remaining what he actually was and is, it will be the province of Natural Science to explain and to demonstrate by natural and spiritual law, how, without mystery or miracle, Jesus became the Master *Christos* and so remains to-day.

Natural Science is not the invention of man, more than is the law of gravitation, the law of equilibrium, or the binomial theorem. Man may discover these laws from the phenomena of Nature, and demonstrate their existence and mode of operation like any others.

It is a question of dispassionate and intelligent apprehension and demonstration.

All actual progress of man up to the present time lies along these lines. Beyond this all is conjecture and guess-work. Natural Science, however,  is far more than modern physical science so-called. It includes physical, mental, moral, and spiritual science.

Its *methods* everywhere and at all times are the same.

It may theorize, but never dogmatize, and it must *demonstrate* at every step. Facts must not only support the theorem, but demonstrate the conclusions as inevitable, and the basis of all such actual demonstration must be a verifiable individual experience, with formulated laws and processes for its repetition, just as in physical science, in chemistry, and mathematics. Nothing less than this on any plane or in any department of investigation can enable the individual to declare "*I Know.*"

Demonstration is the sign manual of knowledge; Dogmatism the arrogance of ignorance.

It is impossible to make these radical distinctions too clear and specific.

When this method of Natural Science is applied to the investigation of religions, tradition is separated from fact, dogma from demonstration, miracle from natural law, mythology and folklore are found to be the fabric woven by the imagination of mankind around the receding revelations, deifying their authors, and mingling fact with fable, till the originals become unrecognizable.

Romance and superstition become substitutes for simple Faith, moral law, and social Justice.

To question or to repudiate the dogmas of superstition becomes a "mortal sin," even when the most plain and specific moral or ethical obligations are entirely subverted or reversed by dogmatic authority.

It is thus that the original revelation is subverted and at last overthrown.

From first to last, the whole fabric is claimed to be "sacred and divine," and to question it, "sacrilege" and "profanation of holy things." Thus, that which seemed originally as wings to the toiling, sorrowing children of men, becomes at last a "millstone about the neck," a "burden grievous to be borne."

Then comes protest, repudiation, reform, and usually a new revelation, embodying the primitive faith, and adapting it to modern times and conditions.

This is, in brief, the history of the Avatars of Ancient India, the Buddhas and the Zoroasters of later centuries; of the Greek Orpheus; of the legends and folklore clustering around many of the sages of Israel, and though in a less miraculous fashion, of Confucius and Laotse. But most patent of all does this principle apply to the founder of the Christian religion, because less ancient and more readily verifiable.

Though no new Avatar is yet recognized, the *spirit* of *modern science* does not hesitate to repudiate myth, miracle, and superstition, and to insist on fact and natural law.

# CHAPTER X

## CORROBORATIVE EVIDENCE

The devout and conscientious believers in the Christian Religion of to-day often view with sorrow and alarm the encroachments of modern science.

Unable to prevent these encroachments, they stubbornly resent them. Once admitted, it seems to them that nothing sacred or worthy the name of Religion would remain. To shift to other and more ancient faiths can never be considered at all, for the "higher criticism" and "pragmatism" have left them all in even a worse plight.

It seems to these devout souls like the death of religion itself, and its elimination from the life of man.

The intuitive basis and the intrinsic necessity of religion in some form have already been considered.

This point is often overlooked or ignored by the Iconoclasts.

Their position would seem to be, "Unravel the superstition, disprove the possibility of miracle, and let the deluge come if it must."

Neither pragmatism nor higher criticism has been in any large sense constructive, but more largely destructive. The really spiritual element in all religions, already referred to, is generally lost sight of.

Modern psychology is no nearer a science of the soul, than are folklore and superstition to true religion. It should be recognized and granted once for all that psychology, as a department of modern physical science, has no substitute whatever to offer in the place of Religion.

It is gathering facts, classifying, and labeling psychic phenomena.

Here and there an advanced scientist, like Sir Oliver Lodge, ignores tradition, repudiates orthodox scientific restraints, and steps over the border of actual or implied nihilism.

This smug nihilism with its superior air of scientific wisdom, is often only the opposite pole of the dogmatic certitude of the churchman. Actual knowledge of the human soul is quite as far removed from the one as from the other. Credulity and Incredulity simply annul each other; often make faces at each other; while Progress stalks alone in the middle of the road, a "tramp" or a "vagabond," like Paracelsus, "reading the leaves of the book of Nature," laughing at poverty, fleeing from persecution, yet *knowing*, and "becoming a light to man forever."

The consensus of opinion among the presidents and professors in the leading colleges and universities of this country, their unhesitating and unqualified denial or repudiation of the claims set up by the church regarding revelation and the basic dogmas of the Christian Religion, and which his "Holiness" of the Vatican designates as "Modernism," reveal, not only the "signs of the times," but show indisputably that modern education has shaken itself free from the superstitions of the past, and repudiated the old restraints to free thought and modern progress.

Orthodoxy in religious matters has often nothing to do in determining college curriculums, in the selection of presidents, or in filling the chairs.

Bright young men and women, the advanced students of the schools of to-day, who are to become the leaders of thought and the teachers of to-morrow, find little restraint and no formative element in the creeds and dogmas that in the past have been so much in evidence, and so constraining. Intensity of feeling has given place to breadth and inclusiveness, and under the name of "Comparative Religions," ancient faiths and modern, are classified, and studied like fossils in the different ages of the past.

The "crusader impulse" has rather settled down in each individual breast, as the master passion, to do, to dare, and to become something more and better than the individual, or than the past has hitherto known. Such a general period of intellectual activity, with so few restraints, history nowhere else records, and the world has never before known.

Here lie the elements, the impulses, and the formative stage of the new Avatar.

At this stage of our discussion it is of exceeding interest and importance to bear in mind one great fact. The average intelligent student of to-day may take this fact tentatively, reserving final judgment till accumulative evidence becomes satisfactory and conclusive.

No one who is dominated by shallow incredulity, and who attempts to close this door contemptuously, will ever arrive at the real truth. The judgment of such individuals is simply worthless, notwithstanding the smug conceit of their own opinions.

The important fact referred to, is the demonstrated existence, all through the ages, of the so-called *Mysteries*.

Their existence is beyond all question. What they concealed and taught is sometimes difficult to determine.

There were also the genuine and the spurious Mysteries, and a fair appreciation of their origin, purpose, methods, and genius, as illustrated by Plato, Pythagoras, Zoroaster, and nearly every great sage of antiquity, leaves no possible doubt that in these "Secret Orders" were preserved the loftiest and the most profound mental and spiritual achievements of all previous human history.

If there were no other evidence in existence at the present day except the traditions, landmarks, ritual, and Genius of Freemasonry, a careful and intelligent study of that Ancient Order would be sufficient.

Whether one Mason in a thousand to-day apprehends and realizes this fact, has nothing whatever to do with the real question. The evidence is there, and the indifference or superficial intelligence of numbers cannot alter it.

# CHAPTER XI

## CONCEPTIONS AND PORTENTS OF AN AVATAR

The conflict between Science and Religion has been thoroughly thrashed out during the last half century, and the "reign of law," and orderly, and progressive evolution, have made for themselves a habitation and a name that nothing is likely to overthrow.

It is recognized that every effect has a sufficient and a commensurate cause, not *en bloc*, but in matter, energy, mind, and spirit. Action and reaction are definite mathematical processes. The parallelogram of force tends everywhere to equilibrium and secures further action and new processes under universal law.

The "special creation" theory—everything made out of nothing by a personal God—is no longer regarded as tenable by intelligent individuals, though miracle and special providence are often included in accounting for the vicissitudes of life, just as the so-called scientist superficially and flippantly uses the word "coincidence," as though it really explained anything.

"The rational order that pervades the universe," as Prof. Huxley defined the concept and aim of scientific discovery, has steadily gained ascendancy, until it dominates and measures individual intelligence.

The criticism is still occasionally made that this means Pantheism, overlooking the fact that in all mythologies and cosmologies, an ideal and pure theism was recognized as lying back of and beyond the pantheons of the gods and the deification of the powers of Nature.

This was true in the Greek, Persian, Egyptian, and Hindoo mythologies. Back of the many, and beyond the transient and contending divinities, was the *One*, postulated, but unknown and changeless.

Every religion known to man, with the advancing civilization of a people, copied, modified, adopted, and adapted the mythology and folklore of some pre-existing religion and people. This is readily demonstrable with the Hebrew, Greek, and later Christian dispensations, notwithstanding the most strenuous and persistent determination to deny, disprove, and destroy the ancient records.

It is embodied in the etymology of the very names of heroes, gods, and demigods. A new language arising with any people *de novo* can nowhere be found.

Phonetics and picturegraphs, the various alphabets and glyphs, are mixed and modified, but never invented nor altogether changed.

Complicated as they may be, it is thus that philology, ethnology, theology, and anthropology constitute a consistent whole, the mythology and folklore of mankind. This reveals the practical unity and solidarity of the human race.

The tradition and prophecy among the ancient Hebrews of the coming of the Messiah, the portents that heralded, and the signs and wonders that preceded or accompanied his appearance, are merely translations or adaptations from previous eras, Buddhas, or Avatars.

Whether Christian or non-Christian, the object of the advent is always identical.

The light of the spirit having become enfeebled or obscured, the people are left in darkness and given over to sin and wickedness. Moral ruin seems inevitable unless there is a divine influx, a new Avatar, or Buddha, or Advent of the God-man.

God incarnates himself as the son of Mary, and Jesus says, "I am come a light into the world that whosoever believeth in me should not abide in darkness."

Christna says, "Though I am unborn, and my nature is eternal, and I am the Lord also of all creatures, yet taking control of my nature-form, I am born by my illusive power. For whenever piety decays, O son of Bharata, and impiety is in the ascendant, then I produce myself. For the protection of good men, for the destruction of evildoers, for the re-establishment of piety, I am born from age to age." (Bhagavadgita.)

The historical Buddha taught that he was only one of a long series of Buddhas, who appear at intervals in the world, and who all teach the same system. After the death of each Buddha his religion flourishes for a time and then decays, till at last it is completely forgotten and wickedness and violence rule the earth. The names of twenty-four of these Buddhas who appeared previous to Gautama have been handed down to us, just as the "second coming of Christ" is believed in and referred to among the Christians.

Even the Mohammedan Koran refers to this succession of prophets and messengers of Allah. The same is true of the Parsis.

"I have said that I first of all chose Abad, and after him I sent thirteen prophets in succession, all called Abad. By these fourteen prophets the world enjoyed prosperity."

"Tradition informs us that when these auspicious prophets and their successors behold evil to prevail among mankind, they invariably withdraw from among them—as they could not endure to behold or hear wickedness."

This is precisely what happened to Egypt after the ambitious priesthood had gained the ascendency. The Master Builders retired.

Bonwick says ("Egyptian Belief and Modern Thought"): "What is commonly called the *Christ idea* of humanity, thus appears to have been the hope and consolation of the ancient Egyptians so many thousand years ago."

That which thus appears and disappears, dies out and is born again, is the spiritual light in the soul of man.

The diversity of man's intellectual activities exercise, elaborate, and deepen his mental perceptions, and these largely concern the things of sense and time, his appetites, passions, desires, and ambitions.

Back of and beyond all these lie the things of the spirit. On the physical plane of life the former obscure and crowd out the latter, which are thus continually in need of renewal.

In adapting the new revelation to the conditions of life on the physical plane, it is intellectualized and theologized. Pundits and theologians undertake to *explain* what it all means and how it happened to be. Hence arise wrangles, disputes, and finally creeds, dogmas, and persecution.

"Men fight like devils for the love of God." This is the ultimate history of every religion known to man.

Meantime, the soul of man, a spiritual being dwelling in a material body on the physical plane, is seeking real knowledge of spiritual things.

This real knowledge is an experience of the soul. It concerns, and is comprised in, the *living of a life*. It is more than mind or intellect. It is *knowledge* gained by experience. "This only I know, that whereas I was blind, now I see."

"Whether in the body or out of the body, I know not, but I saw things impossible to utter."

Gradually man's *idea* of God and his conception of Nature have changed and enlarged.

Man, as a spiritual being, is part of a spiritual universe. He has been able to harmonize his concept of God and Nature progressively as he has gained larger views and deeper insight of both. He is no longer a puppet of infinite caprice, nor a somewhat "improved animal."

The idea of man as a "fallen god" with the capacity to regain his heavenly estate, is far nearer the truth.

As man advances in knowledge through the combined experiences of his spiritual nature and his physical embodiment, his beliefs change, his horizon enlarges, and his concepts become elevated and purified. The past is apprehended and utilized and the future intelligently anticipated. He begins to understand.

This means the recognition of law and order, permanency, *Foundation*, and stability.

The birth stories, the portents, signs and wonders that announce, accompany, or follow the birth of a Messiah or Avatar, are almost identical. A common instinct seems to have led all scripture-compilers to infer a simultaneous stimulus of nature and man upon the appearance of what the Hindoo calls an Avatar.

Men, too, seem prepared to expect such an advent as its necessary time approaches. It is an instinct which tells them that "the darkest hour precedes the dawn."

In the Christian scriptures the premonitions and birth stories are found largely in the Apocryphal books. Doubtless the copying and substitution from the lives of Christna and Buddha were too plain.

At the death of Jesus the seismic, astral, and cosmic disturbances are graphically described, as befitting the death of a god. "The veil of the temple was rent in twain," etc.

The simple fact is that mankind feels instinctively in the soul the far-reaching influences at work. The spiritual nature is stirred to its depths, and when he tries to describe what he sees and feels, his emotions, fears, or aspirations being at white heat, his imagination draws from the folklore of other times, races, and religions, to express what he so powerfully, but vaguely senses.

But beyond all this, the time of great religious revivals and social upheavals is likely to coincide with seismic disturbance, tidal waves and the like, owing to the conjunction of planets under the general law of cycles. Man is completely involved with and evolved from the bosom of Nature. His freedom is determined by knowledge and obedience to Law.

From the mystic Hymns of Orpheus, with the legends of Gods, demigods, and heroes, and the personification of the varied powers of man and nature, arose the Greek Pantheon, which, in poetic concept, romantic and dramatic embodiment and expression, as a concise and complete whole, has probably never been equaled by man.

True, every essential element, under a different name and detail, may be found elsewhere, but never equaled in concise and constructive folklore and mythology.

But running underneath all this, like a vein of gold under the mountain, was the philosophy of Plato. Grasping the *One* from the many, Unity from the fantastic diversity, he came to the individual experience of the human soul and its conscious mastership over the body and the things of sense and time.

Civic pride, patriotism, and heroism, walked side by side with dialectics, and the pantheon of the gods and the achievements of warriors rivaled each other on the stage, as themes for the poetic philosopher and dramatist.

Mythology and folklore here furnished a background from which the philosophy of the mysteries and the real science of life gained a hearing.

Plato and Pythagoras generalized, and with many reservations represented that which they had been taught in the mysteries of Egypt.

Greece, with its triumphs in literature, in the drama and in art, and all its magnificent civilization, knew no Avatar.

Jacolliot, in his "Bible in India," has shown conclusively that not only the whole Greek pantheon, its folklore and mythology, and even its civil code were adopted from the Laws of Manu and the far older Aryan civilization, including even the names of heroes.

The fame of Greece rests upon its *Genius for 159 Construction* in Art and Architecture and the Drama, and upon the open door it gave to Philosophy. There was no dominant priesthood to close the door of progress.

It utilized all the past and built and beautified the present.

It bequeathed no creed nor dogma to the future, and yet its civilization was transcendent and is immortal.

It had its canons of Art and of Architecture. These it demonstrated by constructive work. It illustrated, explained and exemplified, but it did not argue nor dogmatize.

The world for two thousand years has been "going back to Greece" and trying to explain how it all happened, just as we have been trying to explain Goethe's "Faust."

Genius is transcendent and immortal.

With the decline of Greece there arose the Genius of the Tiber, Imperial Rome, and the Cæsars.

Rome created an *Avatar* out of the "Babe of Bethlehem." Having enthroned Jehovah, it proceeded to deify Jesus, and then by substitution to take the place of both.

Imperial Rome, the "Scarlet Mother of the Tiber," assumed the government and dictatorship of the world. Imperial, dogmatic, relentless, the arbiter of the fate of humanity on earth and beyond.

Here was arbitrary, relentless *power* at any cost, to be maintained on any terms. "The end always justified the means."

In the civilization of Greece, the Individual, the citizen was first, and association and co-operation built the State.

With Rome the Individual is nothing but a pawn, an accessory to the Church. It was and is the Church first, last, and all the time. The Individual can claim no right nor prerogative except as a concession from the Church.

The contrast is extreme and absolute between the Genius of Greece and that of Rome.

As the Genius of Greece was adapted from the older Aryan, so also was that of Rome, from the Brahmans, through Egypt.

Among the various Avatars of old India designated as "Incarnations of Vishnu," Siva *"the destroyer,"* was often in evidence.

Rome proceeded to adopt the Hindoo Trinity—Brahma, Vishnu, and Siva—(the Creator, the Preserver, and the Destroyer), and to so shape its creed and dogmas as to secure and maintain the power of Mother Church, simply with a change of names—"Father, Son, and Holy Ghost."

It has enslaved nations and slaughtered millions in order to maintain its power. For more than fifteen hundred years it has maintained its relentless warfare against the inalienable rights of the Individual, and the inevitable progress of humanity.

It has escaped the execration of the world only by its priestly trick of deifying Jesus and sophisticating every doctrine that he taught. Supporting its pretensions by Mariolatry, the Auricular Confession, and its army of spies and inquisitors, it has dominated mankind, impoverished whole nations, devastated provinces and murdered all who opposed its progress wherever and whenever it has gained civil power.

Rome is to-day the literal and visible reincarnation of *Siva*, the *Avatar of Destruction*. She has originated nothing. Her mass and all her ritualistic mummeries are adopted from paganism at its worst stage and in its most degenerate form, and she awaits the fate that befell Egypt and all her predecessors, "Sodom, Gomorrah, and the cities of the plain."

Protestantism has hitherto "protested" only in part. Refusing Mariolatry and auricular confession, Protestantism, by accepting the miraculous conception, the deification of Jesus and the vicarious atonement, has kept Rome in countenance.

When these are swept away, and their doom is already declared by the leaders of thought in nearly all our institutions of higher learning, the Roman *Avatar* will stand revealed in all its nakedness and villainy to the execration of mankind. It is this "*Modernism*" that "His Holiness" so much fears and is trying to arrest. It is too late, unless civilization and the march of time move backward.

The most amazing thing about it all is, how the world, with its present intelligence and culture, can be so indifferent to this most aggressive, cruel, and relentless Avatar of all the ages, instead of repelling it with contempt and execration.

Thirty-seven Italian Cardinals, proud and arrogant, rule the Church, elect the Pope, and assume dictatorship of the earth, as also arbiters of human destiny, here and hereafter. America, the corn-bin of this modern Egypt, by courtesy has *one cardinal*, just to keep her in countenance.

The effrontery is cyclopean, but our supineness and indifference are deplorable and inexcusable.

Shipping her impoverished, degraded, criminal, and priest-ridden hordes to America by the million every year, Rome is massing her army for the overthrow of our government and all our present civilization. With her dogma of obedience, her army now *votes* and will, by and by, *fight* under the dictatorship of the Cardinals at Rome. Already undermining our Public Free Schools, boycotting the public press, with their army of Jesuit spies and secret assassins of every liberty prized by man, the "merry war" goes on right under our eyes, and we sleep and dream and blindly assume that "there is no danger."

Read the history of the Crusaders, of the Protestant Reformation and of the "Holy Inquisition," and if further enlightenment is needed, study the origin, history, and denouement of all the Avatars of the past, the fate of Egypt, the cities of the plain, where paganism and a degenerate priesthood usurped the place of pure and undefiled religion, and literally wiped from the map of the world the civilizations of the past. *Nemesis* is written in letters of flame across the starry heavens, as an atonement for the blood of nations and the degeneracy and diabolism of an ambitious, cruel, relentless, and unrestrained priesthood. And it is all being literally repeated to-day without the novelty of a new idea, or method, or device, or motive. It is *The Reincarnation of the Avatar of Siva, the Destroyer*.

# CHAPTER XII

## PORTENTS OF THE PRESENT TIME

There is no disguising nor denying the fact that during the past half century institutional religion in the West has steadily lost its hold upon the great mass of the people. Creeds and dogmas are denied and repudiated.

The "higher criticism" represents the reluctant yielding of theologians to the existing conditions. In order to maintain any hold whatever upon the people and retain a semblance of the old faith, they have revised and modified beliefs and interpretations, and relaxed completely the former demand for the confession of faith and acceptance of the old creeds. Mere general verbal assent admitting of many mental reservations is now often deemed sufficient.

In the meantime, the living of the life and the doing of the work demanded by Jesus have come more and more into demand and general recognition.

The "Emmanuel Movement," now gaining such recognition and making such rapid progress, is sufficient evidence at this point.

With the Church of Rome no such change is manifest. By keeping its people in ignorance, by  condemning all change or any improvement under the name of "Modernism," and by insisting upon the dogma of infallibility and blind obedience, Rome thus far has resisted all change and refused all compromise.

The change in Protestantism represents the growth of intelligence, the recognition of the rights of conscience, and individual and intellectual freedom.

The stability so apparent in Romanism relies solely on Ignorance, Superstition, and Fear, enforced by the dogma of "*Infallibility*," and reinforced by the power of "Excommunication" and the penalty of "Anathema."

The unity and stability of the Roman Church, thus secured by force, will presently be found to be apparent only. It could only work and hold in the dark ages. Internal division and dissension, now known to exist, await only some fresh act of oppression, or some new abomination, or abuse of political power, to disrupt its solidarity.

In the meantime physical science has steadily advanced, opening new avenues of wealth, industry, and opportunity, and so developing the resources of this Western world.

But more important and far-reaching still have been the discoveries regarding the finer forces of nature.

The wonderful development and application of discoveries in Electricity have not only opened a new world previously unknown and unsuspected, but have seemed to endow these subtle forces almost with an intelligence of their own. Crass materialism is dead and space practically annihilated.

If a single wire or a vibrating disc cannot originate intelligent speech, it can retain, repeat, and transmit the qualities, tones and inflections of the human voice in a way that seems miraculous and uncanny. It is thus that our concepts of nature have been enlarged, refined, and actually spiritualized. "Brutal" and "dead" matter are no longer in evidence nor even mentioned.

With the advent of modern spiritualism came another group of phenomena. Making the largest allowance for fraud, self-deception, and all the vagaries of the imagination, no intelligent individual, familiar with the phenomena, will attempt to deny the extension of man's psychic world of consciousness and the manifestation of intelligence in ways and under conditions previously unknown. The identification of these intelligences, always difficult, and generally problematical, need not here be discussed at all. The facts and the phenomena are all that we are here concerned with.

The most important consideration regarding all these phenomena is that they do not *develop*, but on the contrary *dominate* the individual. They are, in fact, altogether subjective. The medium may put himself in the negative or passive condition to be controlled, but he cannot *command* nor *control* the influence nor the "entity" that influences him, and eventually he loses the power to resist it, and likewise the power of self-control.

Science demands *facts*, and here are facts in abundance. These facts supplement the discoveries in electricity and nature's finer forces, and pass from physics to metaphysics, from physiology to psychology, and push back the veil of the unseen, and hitherto unknown, many degrees.

The trend of all this progress, and of these discoveries, is exceedingly plain.

Our concepts of Nature, of Life, and of Man have been almost immeasurably enlarged, refined, and elevated.

Expectancy is in the air. "What next is going to happen?" is the question everywhere asked. The conditions and portents, in a general way, are those that herald a new

Avatar; an Avatar now, of science rather than of religion; of knowledge rather than of faith, and this knowledge is to be of spiritual things, the foundations of which are already in evidence.

This science is not to be time-serving, but man-serving; not so much a renewal of faith as a revelation of knowledge; less anxious for the glory of God than for the elevation of man, which is the more direct and certain way of honoring Divinity.

This does not mean the decay nor the repudiation of religion, but a *realization* of *true* religion, such as heretofore prophets have foretold, revelation has forecast, and toward which humanity has toiled and journeyed in sorrow and pain; the very religion that Jesus lived and taught. "A clean life, an open mind, an unveiled spiritual perception, a brotherliness for all, and human life a journeying upward toward the realms of eternal day, 'with no night there, and no sorrow.'"

*And why not?* If man can conceive it, why may he not *realize* it? The "Old Adam" as an excuse is exploded. The "New Adam" is indeed "a quickening spirit."

Nothing is plainer nor more demonstrable at the present day than the fact that mankind is slowly but surely shaking off the traditions and the superstitions that have bound it in the past, rising above the myths and the folklore of every age and clime, and awaking as if from slumber, to behold a new day and a new world.

This awakening is even more in evidence and remarkable in the case of woman than of man. Progress here during the last decade has been such as the world has never before seen on any such scale, and it means more to the elevation

165

of humanity than anyone has hitherto been able to forecast or to measure.

In the meantime social and economic conditions with the great masses of the people are very far from what they should be.

Unrest and confusion are strongly in evidence. On the whole, there is far less suffering and destitution than ever before. Oppression and abominations meet with quick and powerful protest from all classes, when exposed, and at least temporary relief is quick to follow.

The blame is confined to no one class, rich or poor. The equitable distribution of wealth, resources, and opportunity that have developed beyond all precedent during the last half century, requires time. Justice and equity are not dead, but everywhere in evidence, dominating mankind at large. Public sentiment was never more keen and never nearer right than to-day. There is general confusion, however, as to methods and ways and means. The cunning shark and the selfish brute resort to concealment, cunning and subterfuge, to deceive the people and often succeed for a time, only to meet with condemnation and execration later. Injustice is often in evidence, but it is neither rampant nor dominant. It stands in fear of public sentiment.

These, in brief and in outline, are the conditions, the portents, to-day, everywhere in evidence:

1. The decay of creeds and dogmas.

2. Great progress in Science, Art, and the Crafts.

3. Immense discoveries regarding Nature's finer forces and the psychical powers latent in man.

**4**. Great expectancy as to new revelations.

**5**. Unprecedented increase in wealth and the development of natural resources.

**6**. Enfranchisement of woman, and immense progress as to her rights and opportunities.

. Economic Justice recognized and aimed at, and fortified by public sentiment, with strong efforts to secure and maintain it.

The present age or epoch is not one of darkness,  but of light; not of discouragement, but of hope. It is neither retrograde nor stagnant, but progressive to a degree never before witnessed in the history of man on so large a scale and involving all classes and so many people at one time.

Organized or institutional religion alone is on the wane. Evidence and utility are everywhere demanded. Nothing is sacred simply because it is old; nor true merely because it is dogmatically asserted so to be.

Holy books, holy men, and holy days are matters of evidence, and not of blind credence.

What will the new religion—the new revelation—be? and whence will it come?

# CHAPTER XIII

## THE SEPARABLE SOUL IN FOLKLORE

Belief in a separable soul in man is virtually universal. Such belief is found amongst the lowest races, and in the few instances where it has not been clearly discovered it is admitted that it may still exist and be disguised by the native meaning of words or signs that escape the explorer.

The universality of this belief has often been urged as an evidence of its validity and proof of the soul's existence.

Modern physical science deduces this belief from the phenomena of daily life and the analogies of individual experience, thus giving precedence to material causes for mental concepts, or universal ideas. This view is, I think, entitled to the most careful consideration, but it cannot once for all be admitted, nor is it consistent with the general theory and progress of evolution that the phenomenal stands to the noumenal, the actual to the ideal, as cause to effect. These two groups of experiences are alternate and coincident; and, as to priority, it is only the old question in a new form, as to which was first, the bird that laid the egg, or the egg that hatched the bird.

This distinction is particularly pertinent to the  present subject, for the reason that by the method of modern physical science, in dealing with the belief in the existence of the soul, the whole of this universal belief is swept away. Its origin is found in the ignorance, superstition, and false analogies of barbarous races, and the inference is that the belief can only linger as a remnant of superstition among civilized men. This method prejudges the whole question, and (while it must readily be admitted that the opposite method equally prejudges it), my contention is for neither the one nor the other, but for the careful consideration and final blending of both. If at first sight these two theories, which form the basis of the working hypothesis of the materialist and the spiritist, seem paradoxical and wholly irreconcilable, with careful consideration and unbiased investigation of both sides of the problem the paradox will disappear.

With both the lowest and the highest races not only do we find the existence of belief in the existence of a separable soul in man, but of ghosts, gods, genii, a spirit of the air, and hierarchies of celestial and infernal beings.

In this regard, philosophers like Plato and Pythagoras, the intellectual giants of the human race, may be said to have elaborated and specialized the rude conceptions of the Fiji Islander, and to vie with him in peopling space with invisible entities and potencies. In spite of the dictum of science, the world, intelligent and ignorant alike, believes, and will continue to believe, in the reality of the unseen universe, and the Platonic doctrine of "emanation" and the "world of divine ideas" not only begin where modern physical science leaves off, but at this very point science either begs the question, or ignores it entirely.

How things come to be what they are, and to evolve as they do, science nowhere declares. It simply takes things as it finds them, and dubs the ultimate and antecedent causation the *Unknowable*. The philosophy of Plato, it is true, reaches at last the unknowable and the incomprehensible, but only after revealing another universe, the metaphysical and spiritual, entirely unknown to, or ignored or derided by the materialist.

It is, however, from this invisible realm that all visible things have come forth, the two being not only under absolute and universal law, but bearing everywhere definite analogies to each other. Hence Plato says, "God geometrizes." Absolute mathematics determines the relations of atoms to suns, and the circulation of the blood in man to the revolutions of suns and solar systems.

A further general consideration remains to be noted before taking up the evidence of belief in the separable soul, and that is, the evolutionary life-wave of humanity on our earth.

The progress of man for some millions of years past has by no means been a straightforward climbing from barbarism to civilization. The wave of evolution has ebbed and flowed. While at one place man has slowly emerged from savagery, at another he has as surely sunk to it. Continents and islands have risen from and again sunk to the bottom of the sea, bearing the races of men in their upheavals or descent, and cataclysmic and seismic or volcanic upheavals have blotted out in a day the accumulated progress of centuries. The poles of the earth have shifted with results to the life of the globe more awful than the imagination can portray. Bodies of people like our North American Indians represent the remains of many peoples, as in Russia or India to-day, fragments of many nationalities are being absorbed in one.

Bearing in mind, therefore, that owing to many causes a nation may descend to barbarism or disappear entirely, we shall find everywhere the fragments and decay of the old belief no less than the dawn of the new. A noble creed, or a philosophical concept of a highly advanced race, may exist as a transformed and degrading superstition with a race, or a fragment of a people, undergoing degeneracy.

Every religion known to man has gone through just this transformation. The tendency is innate and inevitable and no civilization or religion has ever yet been able long to resist it. If we bear this in mind we shall be less surprised at anthropogeneses, cosmogeneses or psychologies found sometimes among otherwise rude or savage peoples, and be better able to understand the incongruities and lack of symmetry in their evolution. It would be  easy to cite instances and draw comparisons at this point.

Bearing in mind, then, these general considerations underlying all interpretation, and nowhere more applicable than to our present subject, the following illustrations of belief in the separable soul, gleaned largely from Spencer's "Descriptive Sociology," may be of interest. It is drawn largely from the lower civilizations, as all are more or less familiar with the mythologies of the Greeks, Babylonians, Phœnicians, etc., all of which are accessible. The material available is embarrassing on account of its magnitude alone.

Oscar Peschel, in his "Races of Man," says that "perhaps the Brazilian Botocudos, of all the inhabitants of the world, are most nearly in the primitive state, and yet," he adds, "possibly we may be altogether mistaken in this regard, as their languages are very imperfectly known."

Humboldt rescued the Caribs from such an impeachment and declares that their language "combines wealth, grace, strength, and gentleness. It has expressions for abstract ideas, for Futurity, Eternity, and Existence, and enough numerical terms to express all possible combinations of our numerals." It might be noted in passing that it was these same Brazilian natives that the Portuguese settlers sought to decimate by spreading smallpox and scarlet fever amongst them, as the English colonists in Tasmania shot the natives when they had no better food for their dogs.

Hariot says that "many of the Indian natives of North and South America believe that the soul, after its separation from the body, enters into a wide path crowded with spirits which are journeying toward a region of eternal repose. They have to cross an impetuous river on a trembling wicker bridge which is very dangerous."

Some Greenlanders believe that the soul can go astray out of the body for a considerable time. Some believe that they can leave their souls at home when going on a journey, and others believe in the migration of souls.

Belief in the soul and a future state is universal among the Indians of North America. All are familiar with the tradition of the "Happy Hunting Ground." With them the future life is patterned after the present.

Schoolcraft says that the Chippewas believe that there are duplicate souls, one of which remains with the body, while the other is free to depart on excursions during sleep. After death the soul departs to the Indian Elysium and a fire is kept burning on the newly-made grave for four days, the time required for the soul to reach its destination.

The Dakotas stand in great fear of the spirits of the dead, who they think have power to injure them, and they recite prayers and give offerings to appease them.

The Mandans, according to Schoolcraft, have anticipated Prof. Lloyd's Etidorhpa, even to the beautiful maiden. They believe that they were the first people created on the earth, and that they first lived inside the globe. They raised many vines, one of which having grown up through a hole in the earth, one of the young men climbed up until he crawled out on the bank of the river where the Mandan village stands. (Jack and the bean stalk.) The young man returned to the nether world and piloted several of his companions to the outer world, and among them two very beautiful virgins. Among those who tried to get up was a very large and fat woman, who was ordered by the chiefs to remain behind. Her curiosity prompted her secretly to make the trial. The vine broke under her weight and she was badly hurt by the fall, but did not die, and was ever after in disgrace for having cut off all communication with the upper world. Those who had already ascended built the Mandan village, and when these die they expect to return to the nether world from which they came. They also believe the earth a great tortoise, and have a tradition of a universal deluge.

The Indians of Guiana believe in the immortality of the soul, as do also the Arawaks. The Brazilians are said by Spix and Martins to have had no religious belief whatever before mingling with the civilized races. The Guaranis believed in a soul which remained in the grave with the body.

The Patagonians believe in a country of the dead which they call Alhue Mapu and they kill the horses of the deceased in order that their owner may ride in Alhue Mapu.

From the beliefs of the Negritto and Malayo-Polynesian races, I glean the following: The Fuegians believe in a superior being, and in good and evil spirits, in dreams, omens, signs, etc. Fitzroy says he could not satisfy himself that they had any idea of the immortality of the soul.

The Veddahs believe in the guardianship of the spirits of the dead, who visit them in dreams and minister to them in sickness, and they have ceremonies of invocation.

Eyra says some at least of the Australians believe in the existence and separability of the soul.

The Tasmanians believed in a future life as a tradition of a primitive religion, and Bonwick says they conversed with the spirits of the dead.

The New Caledonians believe that white men are the spirits of the dead, and that they bring sickness. They believe that the soul on leaving the body goes to the Bush, and every fifth month they have a "spirit night" or "grand concert of spirits." The gods of the New Caledonians are their ancestors, whose relics they keep and idolize.

The Fijians believe in a separable soul, and dying is by them described by the same terms as sunset.

Belief in a future state among them is said by Siemann to be universal. In Fiji heaven the inhabitants plant, live in families, fight, and so repeat the incidents of life on earth. They believe that the spirit of men, while still alive, may leave the body and trouble other people when asleep.

The Sandwich Islanders believe that the spirit of the departed hovers about his former home, appears to his relatives in dreams, and they worship an image which they believe to be in some way connected with the departed. They regard the spirit of one of their ancient kings as a tutelar deity, and the king and the priest were believed to be descended from the gods.

The Tahitians believe in a separable soul which, on leaving the body, is seized by other spirits and conducted to the state of night, where it is by degrees eaten by the gods. A few escape this fate, while others, after being three times eaten, become immortal.

The Tongons believe that the human soul is the more ethereal part of the body and that it exists in Bolotoo in the form and likeness of the body the moment after death.

The Samoans believe that the spirits of the dead have power to return and to cause disease and death in other members of the family, hence all are anxious to part with the dying on good terms.

The New Zealanders believe that during sleep the mind leaves the body, and that dreams are the objects seen during its wanderings. They believe in two separate abodes for departed spirits, the sky, and the sea, and that the abodes of souls are to be approached only down the face of a steep precipice—Cape Maria Van Dieman.

The Dyaks have great difficulty in distinguishing sleep from death. They believe that the soul during sleep goes on an expedition of its own, and sees, hears, and talks. They believe in spirits, omens, and in all that occurs in dreams as real and literally true.

The Sumatrans believe in spirits and superior beings, and are said to have a vague idea of the immortality of the soul, and the Malays believe in spirits, good and bad, and seem to have a vague idea of a separable soul.

The Mexicans believed in a separable soul, and distinguished three different abodes for it after death.

Landa says the people of Yucatan have always believed more firmly in the immortality of the soul than other people, though they were less advanced in civilization. They believed that after death there would be a better life, which the soul would enjoy after its separation from the body. They worshiped their dead kings as gods. The mythology of the people of Guatemala, Honduras, and Nicaragua is extensive and complicated and their National Book, the Popol Vuh, possesses intense interest for the student. There can be no doubt that these people believed in a separable soul, as did also the Chibchas.

It was the belief of the ancient Peruvians that the soul leaves the body during sleep, and that the soul itself cannot sleep, but that dreams are what the soul sees in the world while the body sleeps. Waitz says they believed in the transmigration of human souls into the bodies of animals.

In the case of the Arabians the primitive belief, which was Sabianism, has been altered far less by Mohammedan invasion than most persons suppose. Burton says Mohammed and his followers conquered only the more civilized Bedouins, and Baker says that the Arabs are unchanged, and that the theological opinions which they now hold are the same as those which prevailed in remote ages, and of this belief the soul and its immortality formed a part.

In general the Hill Tribes of India share in the universal belief in the soul, in spirits, gods, and devils, though of many of these tribes little is really known in modern times.

Nearly all our North American Indians (I can find no exceptions) bury objects with their dead, such as food implements, jewelry, etc., and kill the horses of the deceased that he may ride in the Happy Hunting Ground.

With the Carib's death his wife and captives were killed, and food utensils, etc., were buried with him.

A curious custom prevailed with some Brazilian tribes. After burying food, utensils, arms, etc., with the body, a month after death the body was disinterred, put in a pan over a fire, the volatile substances driven off, the black residue reduced to powder and mixed with water and drunk by the company.

The Patagonians bury all the possessions of the deceased with the body.

With the Hottentots, widows lose one joint of a finger as an offering to the deceased husband every time they re-marry.

With the Kaffirs, the hut and utensils of the deceased are burnt. The East Africans offer prayer to the dead.

The Congo people bury ornaments, utensils, arms, etc., and embalm the body after one or two years. The body of the chief must be carried in a straight line from the hut to place of burial, and if trees or huts impede the passage, they are cut down.

The Coast Negroes bury property with the body and have a ceremony like an Irish wake, as do also the Abyssinians.

With the Ashantis, gold dust and utensils are buried and human sacrifices occur.

The wives of the Fijians are strangled that they may attend their lords in the new country.

The people of Malagasy bury in vaults **10×12**, and **7** feet high, and put in a large quantity of property.

With the ancient Mexicans, wives, slaves, concubines, and chaplains were slaughtered to attend the deceased.

The Arabs fasten the camels to the grave of their master.

The Todas cremate the dead and slaughter the whole herd of buffalo belonging to him, in order to secure them to him in the after life.

I have by no means given a complete category of the primitive and barbarous peoples who believe in a separate soul, and who believe in a future state much like the present and in conformity with that belief bury arms, ornaments, and utensils with the dead or place them on the grave, and who slaughter horses, camels, wives, slaves, etc., in order that the deceased may retain his possessions. How far these customs extend in case of the death of woman I do not know, but as with most of these people the women are regarded as chattels of the males, the case is doubtless very different.

Now as to the origin of these beliefs and customs, their causes naturally fall into two categories, the physical and the metaphysical. Modern biological science regards the whole question from the physical side almost exclusively, and facts and experiences that belong largely or exclusively to the metaphysical realm are warped out of their natural order to fit the theory of interpretation.

Every savage observes not only that he casts a shadow, but that shadows attend all inanimate objects that stand so as to intercept the light, and as shadows move as do objects that gives rise to the idea of animation. Hence we have genii, dryads, naiads, ghosts, angels, demons, etc. To fortify this belief we have echoes, which give voice to animate and inanimate objects. Movement and voice are the universal accompaniment of animation.

The part played by the breath, and its sudden cessation at death, are believed to contribute to the belief in invisible existences.

The beating of the heart, and its cessation at death, adds another link to the chain of phenomena, going to show that *something* leaves the body at death. This may be the origin of the sacrifice of the hearts of captives to the gods, or to a deceased warrior or chief as with the ancient Mexicans, with the belief that the heart is the seat of the soul, and the soul of the captive or victim shall attend the departed chief in the other world.

But the most important place should doubtless be assigned to dreams as giving rise to belief in the world of spirits. Dreams are universal amongst men, and animals like the dog also dream.

Most if not all primitive people are also aware that fasting promotes dreaming, and while many of them practice long fasting, partly, no doubt, to increase fortitude and bodily endurance, in very many cases it is known to be practiced for the purpose of promoting dreams. Beyond this voluntary fasting there is the enforced fast due to famine or the scarcity of food.

It will be noticed in many of the cases cited how much stress is laid on the phenomena of dreams and how literally they are interpreted.

Among civilized races and those wise in philosophy dreams play a very important part, and are classified as monitorial, prophetic, etc., etc. The habit in modern times of regarding dreams as altogether fantastic and unreal, is unscientific. In the mingling of the real and the apparently unreal, in the dream state, while the experience itself is always real to the dreamer, lies undoubtedly the source of many beliefs that influence the lives of men.

Dreaming must be regarded as one of the states of consciousness, and hence, of whatsoever stuff dreams are made, they represent an actual experience of the individual. No greater mistake can be made than the belief that no experience is real save that which brings us in contact with gross matter through the agency of the five senses. The world of ideas and the creations of the imagination are in fact no more evanescent than matter itself. Here impermanency differs only in time. All in time pass away.

I hold that dreams, in general, show more clearly the nature of the soul, and the experiences of the waking state show the office of the bodily organism, and that each *on its own plane* is as valid as the other.

In other words, "the soul is such stuff as dreams are made of." It does not hold true, nor need it, that the experiences in dreams shall be true and valid on the physical plane, though this is often the case, or that the experiences of the physical plane shall be literally repeated in dreams, which, nevertheless, frequently happens.

It is an undeniable fact that the experiences of the conscious ego in man compass the subjective no less than the objective planes of being. That the subjective avenues should be closed when the ego is functioning on the physical plane through the bodily organs by aid of the

180

senses, is quite as remarkable as that the physical avenues should be closed when in dreams, or trance, or syncope, or under anaesthetics, the ego functions on the subjective planes.

I hold, therefore, that here, more than anywhere else, is the source of not only belief in the existence of the soul, but of the relatively uniform conceptions everywhere attained. The common experience of man on the one plane is as easily accounted for as on the other, and individual experience differs no more widely in the one case than in the other. So also is the persistence of the human type, or the *genus*, involved in the one case no less than in the other.

All the agencies recognized in modern evolution tend to elevation only through differentiation, and even the "eternal cell" of Weismann fails in explaining permanency of form through any physical transmission. When atavism and degeneracy are admitted as factors, as they certainly must be, the perpetuity of the human species fails from physical causes alone.

I hold the idea of a separable soul to be innate in the human consciousness, as a necessary deduction from the experience of the continuity of self-consciousness which compasses both the objective and subjective states. This deduction from experience occurs whenever the evolving ego has advanced sufficiently above the animal plane to reason on its own experience, and for this reason the belief in the separable soul is universal.

It is no more strange that the experience of the individual should be modified by traditions and the beliefs of others regarding, for example, the dream state, than that the experience of the individual should in like manner be modified or shaped by traditions and the ceremonies and usages of others on the physical plane. The bond of unity and that of diversity have one common root in humanity. What we need for larger knowledge is, I think, a recognition of the breadth and sweep of human experience. To stop either ignoring or quibbling over one-half of all our actual experience.

The inner world of thought and being is really the habitat of the soul, while the physical body, like the diving-bell, enables us to explore and gain experience on another plane which otherwise must remain to us forever unknown.

The limitations of space and time are unknown to us in dreams. These are the limitations of the fleshly casket. The consciousness of freedom, the absence of pain and sorrow even under great trial, are often experienced in the dream state. The range and character of experience in the subjective state is modified, and held in check by that of the physical plane, and the correspondence of an emotion to an idea, or of an act to a thought, ought to give us the key to the two sets of experiences and reveal the underlying basis of equilibrium.

A universal fact and a common experience argue a universal nature. Like conditions everywhere come from like causes. These are neither accidental nor incidental, nor are they left to the caprice of savages, nor to that of the more advanced civilizations.

It is not at all strange that a common experience should result in a universal belief. The range of experience and varying vicissitudes of life on the outer physical plane differ as widely as do those of the dream plane, and the conscious identity of the individual is equally preserved on both planes.

I hold that here lies the origin of belief in the existence of a soul in man, separable from the body, and the confines of matter, space, and time, in an actual experience of every individual. The beating of the heart, the phenomena of respiration, the cessation of these at death, and the shadows cast by man and inanimate bodies serve as connecting links between the experiences of the individual on the subjective and objective planes of being.

The dream state and the experiences thence derived are subjects for psychological science to investigate. The experiences allotted by du Maurier to "Peter Ibbetson" are not altogether fantastic and unwarranted, as the records of somnambulism and hypnotism abundantly prove. When we remember that nothing deserving the name of Psychology or Psychic Science exists in the western world to-day, we need not wonder why men eminent for investigations in other departments prove themselves novices and dogmatists here.

The folklore, the traditions, and the mythology of dreams would form a very interesting subject for discussion. It is true that the literature of the subject is fantastic, mixed with fable and often altogether unreliable; but these difficulties offer no more formidable bar to scientific investigation than many another problem already classified and formulated for systematic study.

I know a lady of very superior ability, the mother of a prominent jurist, who all her life has had distinct premonitions of many calamities and coming events, and there are those who dream true in every community. Fantasies, nightmare, dreams from indigestion and delirium, form a separate class where the dreamer is entangled in the meshes of the bodily functions.

Here fasting, either voluntary or enforced, comes in, and drugs known to the remotest times are found to promote and to determine the character of dreams. There are furthermore processes of mental gymnastics whereby the thinker withdraws himself from the bodily avenues of sense and functions at will on the subjective plane of being.

"When then," said Socrates, in the *Phædo*, "does the soul light on the truth? for when it attempts to consider anything in conjunction with the body, it is plain that it is led astray by it."

"And surely," he continues, "the soul reasons best when none of these things disturb it, neither hearing, nor sight, nor pain, nor pleasure of any kind, but it retires as much as possible *within itself, taking leave of the body*, and as far as it can, not communicating or being in contact with it, *it aims at the discovery of that which is.*"

I hold that the most valuable triumphs of science in the future lie in the realm of psychology, and that by no means the least important contribution in this direction will come from the study of Folklore, of which belief in the separable soul, and the phenomena and universality of the dream state must form a very important part.

One final consideration is suggested not without some degree of hesitation and diffidence. If there be a soul in man destined to continued existence, and if in any case perfection is the goal of evolution as formulated by Herbert Spencer for a future residue of the human race, then this soul in its essential elements is without beginning in time.

Pre-existence and evolution necessitate repeated re-embodiment on the physical plane, and the continuity of self-consciousness in man I hold to be the proof of life without beginning or end.

Viewed in this light, dreams and all subjective experiences in man must mingle reminiscences of the soul with the experiences of the present life, and the theory of innate ideas assumes a purely scientific form. We hence arrive at the intuition of the soul to account for universal belief. The experience of Socrates and the Fiji Islander agree as to the subjective plane as perfectly as in regard to the beating of the heart. They differ only in degree of evolution.

# CHAPTER XIV

## FROM CONFUSION TO CONSTRUCTION

A concise and detailed review of the past, in the long journey of man toward civilization and independent self-knowledge, has not been herein attempted. Only hints, here and there, and the barest outline have been undertaken.

If, however, the intelligent student will follow these clews, he will find a mass of material and abundant evidence to corroborate the general thesis.

Every great religion has had its Avatar, its Redeemer, its *Christos*.

Each of these religions has adapted from its predecessors and transformed the old, in whole or in part, to suit the conditions and apparent needs of the time.

Each of these revivals of religion has been instituted on account of the abominations of a dominant priesthood and the poverty and degradation of the masses. What was at first claimed and instituted as a Divine Revelation for the elevation and happiness of the whole people, has openly and shamelessly degenerated into enslavement of the masses and the creation of a despotic and arrogant class who enslaved both body and soul in the name of Religion.

Priest, Prince, and Potentate generally, united to terrorize through force, and by superstition and fear, in order to retain their power.

The reaction has invariably resulted from economic conditions, as in the case of the Protestant Reformation, when the gold sent to Rome through the shameless sale of Indulgences, threatened to impoverish the whole of Northern Europe, and Princes broke allegiance to the Priesthood in desperate self-protection.

Then, and then only, came sufficient protest and Reformation.

The religionist is apt to regard and designate Science as "profane," and Religion *per se*, as essentially "holy."

Nothing can be really considered "holy" that does not elevate, encourage, and inspire the whole human race and promote the Brotherhood of Man. Whenever any religion fails to do this it becomes indeed a profanation of holy things.

The only religion that ever became the inspiration of a whole people, so far as history records, was that of Christna, with the teeming millions of India. Buddhism was driven out of India by the powerful and unscrupulous Brahmans, and took refuge in Ceylon, Thibet, and adjacent provinces.

The religion of Jesus met a similar fate from the Jews and the Roman governors, until Pagan Rome adapted and transformed it on the principle of dominance and exploitation inherent in the genius of the Latin Race.

Since which time no one will pretend to claim that the Religion of Jesus has ever dominated the human race or any large part of it.

Rome to-day no more represents the religion of Jesus than the Brahmans of to-day represent that of Christna, or Buddha, or the religion of the Vedas.

Nothing is so amazing to-day as that the intelligence of the present age fails to recognize this fact.

All of these religions of the past have adapted their teaching to the multitude through parable and allegory. Nothing in literature can be found more beautiful and inspiring, and at the same time comprehensible to the commonest intelligence, than Christna's "Parable of the Fisherman."

Christna and Buddha, like Jesus, taught to their disciples a "Secret Doctrine," apprehensible only to the few. "To you it is given to know the mysteries," but to others, who are without, it is not given.

It can readily be proven from at least a half score of the early Church Fathers (see page **70** *et seq.* of the author's "Mystic Masonry"), that the early church practiced "Initiation," patterned after those of the Gnostics, Therapeutia and the Mysteries of Egypt, and divided their neophytes and postulants into three degrees, as in Blue Lodge Masonry to-day.

While the great mass of mankind to-day are incapable of apprehending these genuine mysteries of life, and of the individual soul of man, it is doubtful if any civilization ever existed where so many were willing and capable of understanding them as are found here in America to-day.

The reason for this and the growth of intelligence have already been outlined.

A new race is slowly forming here, designated by the ancient Wisdom as the "Fifth Race," and called the *Manasic*, the growth of Intelligence, or "Mind."

It is above all things important that with this development of *Mind* there should also develop that of *Buddhi*, or Loving Kindness, the essential element in the Universal Brotherhood of Man; a thing largely overlooked in the modern theory of Evolution, and ignored, or set at naught by Romanism by its dogmas, anathemas, and persecutions. Instead of the brotherhood of man, she has exhibited the cruelty and rapacity of devils. (Establishment of Roman Catholic Caste.)

This all-around development of the whole man, as essential to human evolution, is everywhere insisted upon by all the great Masters of antiquity, and is illustrated and exemplified in the genuine Greater Mysteries.

Hence, the saying in Kabala, "The wicked *obey* the law through *fear*; the wise *keep* the law through *knowledge*." The Saviors all preached and practiced the "Good Law," and obedience to legal mandates.

The explanation usually given of an Avatar by the ancient Masters, as "a descent, embodiment, or incarnation of *Vishnu*," who is not only the "Preserver," but the "Rejuvenator" of mankind, is rather a *blind*, and was an interpretation given to the common people, or the "profane."

All things—even heaven and earth—pass away, and all things are renewed.

This renewal, or regeneration, through the constructive principle of evolution, is "designed" to be continually on higher and still higher planes.

It is not the range of experience, nor the growth of intelligence alone, that elevates man, but the progressive and constructive growth of the soul, from the physical toward the spiritual plane of Being.

This actual growth means Knowledge, Wisdom, Understanding, Knowledge of the Law, Obedience to its Commands, and Realization of its Rewards.

This Constructive Psychology is the *growth of the Soul*.

Man passes, therefore, from the age of Fable, Superstition, and Fear, to the age of Faith and Obedience, and finally to that of actual Knowledge.

This *age of Knowledge*—not for all of mankind, but for a larger number who are worthy and well-qualified, duly and truly prepared than was ever known at one time before— has at last dawned.

The question is continually asked, "Why do the Masters of Wisdom Conceal their Knowledge?"

The only adequate answer is that so few are ready, willing, and able to receive it in the right way, and to use and not abuse it.

Those who deny that any such knowledge has ever existed, or exists to-day, or can exist, had better waste no time over it. They cannot alter it, nor destroy it, as their predecessors have tried to do for ages, often murdering or crucifying all who were even suspected of possessing it. They might as well try to destroy the law of gravitation, or imagine that by murdering the foremost mathematician of the day that they had destroyed the science of mathematics. I am speaking of *Knowledge* of Spiritual things.

A new Avatar, therefore, is not simply an individual, though many individuals may understand and exemplify it—the Initiated, the Illuminati—and one man may lead in representing it.

To call it "the descent and embodiment, or Incarnation of Vishnu," in a metaphysical sense, the Spirit (generically), that renews, rejuvenates, transforms, and regenerates, is by no means an empty metaphor.

In the same sense we speak of the "Genius of Greece," or of Rome, or of Civilization.

The *idea* is composite, and represents an underlying and *universal principle and potency*.

But after all metaphor and generalization, each Avataric movement centered around an individual *Man*, and this *Man* embodied the principle and undertook the special work of an evangel, or *Christos*, or "Avatar," amongst men.

Not only have there been many Avatars, and many Buddhas, but when we realize the meaning of these terms and the mysteries they represent, we discover that while it may be the special mission of one, like Christna, or Buddha, or Jesus, to undertake the work of enlightening and redeeming any age; there are other Masters, or Illuminati, engaged in other work, on different planes, to promote the same general results.

The result with each of the great Saviors of mankind has been, that the common people, or the priesthood, have eventually either crucified or deified them.

In the case of Jesus they have done both. Eight separate and deliberate attempts have already been made to assassinate the present representative of the School of Natural Science, who was educated in the order of the Illuminati, and delegated by that Order to present these great truths to the world to-day.

This individual is only in the broadest *metaphysical* sense (as already defined), an Avatar, which, as shown, is a *composite idea, focused* in and *represented by* an individual man or teacher.

The work of this Master is to instruct, to exemplify, and to demonstrate, the ancient Wisdom on Scientific lines, in keeping with the needs, the opportunities, and the scientific spirit of the present age.

He does not preach to the multitude in parables. He undertakes to instruct the few who are ready  and qualified to receive such instruction, and who will properly use and not abuse it, and he does this "without money and without price"; "without the hope of fee or reward." (Herein is the Avataric Spirit of Freemasonry.)

What his reward will be with the rabble, or with the "money changers," he knows too well, but to such as he, fear is unknown.

I am speaking not *for* him, but *of* him, after the blessed privilege of seven years of the most intimate association, and such co-operation as I have been capable of giving.

His plan and motive seem to be to get as much as possible of this knowledge of the soul, and of spiritual things, to the attention of the "progressive intelligence of the present age," in order that it may become exemplified and diffused among all classes, and for the benefit of the whole human race.

We have passed the age of fable, and of blind faith, and have come to the age of fact and law. *Kali Yuga* means the Iron Age.

As two natures, the physical and spiritual, meet and mingle in the constitution of man, so do his faculties, capacities, and powers mingle and function on the two planes, the physical and the spiritual, though very largely on the former, with the great majority in any age or time.

There is implanted in the very foundation of man's being the idea or the consciousness of a separable soul. It would seem to be an intuition, for with nearly every people of which we have any knowledge, no matter how near the animal plane, the belief or the folklore of a separable soul exists, in many cases held to be separable during life, and in most cases believed to survive the death of the physical body. (See folio editions of Herbert Spencer's "Descriptive Sociology," and Chapter XIII, herein.)

It has generally been held by scientists and commentators, that this intuition, or belief, results largely from dreams.

To say that dreams, in general, are mere fantasies, or the results of imagination, and have no real basis in consciousness, is folly; for dreams are of many kinds, and present great varieties.

They are, moreover, both reminiscent and prophetic, sometimes moving like any other conscious experience, from fact to fruition, and in others, we are unable to relate them to any other conscious experience.

Hypnosis and Telepathy are related to the same states, so much so, that the modern scientist has been constrained to coin two new terms to avoid endless repetitions, viz.: "subliminal" and "supraliminal" states of consciousness.

Bearing in mind all these subjective states and experiences, including the whole range of so-called mediumship, the *theorem* of the Masters and adepts of all ages may be made exceeding plain.

It consists in the *dominance of the Will* over all conscious states.

This is the *Alpha* and the *Omega*—the principle, the potency, and the act—of Mastership.

The mind of the Master no longer drifts in a boundless sea of fantasy, but with rudder and compass, he guides his ship whithersoever he would go.

This does not mean that there are not still degrees and related states and conditions of consciousness in his experience.

It does mean, however, that all these states and conditions, with all his faculties, capacities, and powers, are *co-ordinated*, not only in his *awareness* of them as a whole, but in the exercise of each and its relation to the others, dominated by his own Will.

He has "Mastered" them, and can incite or repress them, while they can no longer dominate him. Can the reader imagine such a degree of *Self-Control?*

This, however, is but the beginning, as the "Secret of Power," and by no means the end.

Controlling the phases and forms of consciousness, there comes next the determination to extend their boundary and to *refine and elevate the powers of the Soul*.

In the first case, that of co-ordination, the ancient Wisdom admonishes the student or *chela* to "*make the mind one pointed, like a light burning in a quiet place.*" Light a candle and put it in a corner  where no draught can reach it, and the flame will seem as though cut out of solid fire, and "one pointed."

It is at the point of refining and elevating the individual consciousness that Ethics or Morals come in. It is just at this point also that the *Path* is determined.

What our ancient Brothers called "the power of Will and Yoga"—self-control—*may* ignore Ethics. Here the paths separate, and are called "the Right-hand Path" and "the Left-hand Path," determining the "White" and the "Black Magician," about whom so much is said in all ancient scriptures and traditions regarding "Sorcery" and "Black Magic," of which Egypt and Rome and Modern Mediumship and Hypnotism, are illustrations.

The *supreme importance* of this natural division or "parting of the way" reveals the real and final reason why the Masters of the "right-hand path" conceal their knowledge from the profane and reveal it only after an ethical formulary has been learned and once for all *ingrained*.

The "Thugs" of India are no more an idle dream nor a bugaboo to frighten children and old women than are the Mafia and the Roman Jesuit to-day.

In Egypt the time came when these "Black Magicians" dominated the people and drove out those of the right-hand path who built the great pyramid and gave to Egypt the wisdom and glory of its prime.

The consciousness and power of these evil men, however, was limited to the lower planes. Whenever they wished to transcend these lower planes they were powerless. Hence arose the *Sibyl*; young boys or virgins were hypnotized, and being pure, they could thus be inducted into a somewhat higher plane. (See Mabel Collins' "Idyll of the White Lotus.")

Margrave, in Bulwer's "Strange Story," is a fine picture of an "adept of the left-hand path." He would sacrifice the whole human race in order to gain his personal and selfish ends, just as would "Mother Church" to-day.

The Master of the White Lodge would readily lay down his life for the benefit of his fellowmen. Herein is the vital difference.

Here lies the meaning and the complete antithesis represented by *Christos* and *Satan*. Both names are generic and Avataric, and yet, may be personified.

This elevating and refining process to which I have referred is not a matter of sentiment or emotion, but a matter of fact, with a definite, scientific formula.

In a previous chapter belief in the existence AND SEPARABILITY OF THE HUMAN SOUL HAS BEEN SHOWN to be virtually universal, and in some cases, even with people of very low development, the belief is held that the soul may be separated from the body and reunited again during life.

This is, however, a *belief*, and proves nothing as to *fact*, *science*, and *law*, beyond the existence of the belief, with all the appurtenances, concomitants, and subjective experiences of individuals thereunto belonging.

We thus arrive at the real *theorem* as a cold psychological problem.

Can the existence and separability of the soul of man, during his physical embodiment on earth, and its survival of the death of the physical body, be scientifically demonstrated as a *fact*?

If so, then the principles involved, the methods employed and the whole *modus operandi* must be capable of exact, scientific formulation, the same as any other theorem of science.

Furthermore, granting that this is true, and that it can be done according to exact formulary, the value, the effect of such a demonstration upon the character and the normal faculties, capacities, and powers of the individual who undertakes and accomplishes such a demonstration, must be revealed and taken fully into account.

Does it elevate or degrade him? Is it in line with normal evolution, and therefore, potentially the birthright, and finally, through spiritual evolution, the higher destiny of all men?

Nor is this all. The effect of the existence of such Knowledge and of its teaching, upon communities, as a substitute for blind superstition, credulity, or belief, must also be taken into account.

It may thus be seen how much even beyond the mere *fact* of demonstration, is included in this transcendent problem; this question of all ages, "If a man die, shall he live again?" or, "Does the real man ever die at all?"

Now it is a demonstrated fact, proven in every case of a genuine Master, and held inviolable in the "Greater Mysteries" of every age and time, that the ethical question above raised, as to the effect upon individuals and society, *comes first*, and is made a *test* of the "first step" in the way of demonstration.

This is the meaning of the oft repeated quotation, the candidate for initiation must first be "worthy and well-qualified, duly and truly prepared."

This comprises and constitutes the "Lesser Mysteries," as in the School of Pythagoras, viz.: the instruction of the neophyte in ethics or morals.

Nor is this instruction sufficient in any case. The candidate must himself demonstrate that he has absorbed, apprehended, and utilized such instruction by *"Living the Life."*

In other words, it must have become so ingrained in his character as to govern absolutely all his acts and impulses to action, i.e., automatic, habitual, and natural.

In the School of Natural Science this comprises and constitutes the "Ethical Section of the General Formulary."

In the School of Pythagoras we are informed that students sometimes remained for years in the "outer court," and sometimes they failed entirely and hopelessly, and went back to the outer world. Whereupon a white stone was erected to their memory as though they were dead. They were indeed, for the time being, dead to the School.

This fully answers the ethical question as to the effect of this real knowledge on the individual and on mankind.

The real Master sees to it that all that precaution can provide, or human wisdom can suggest, is done to insure beneficent *use* of the knowledge gained.

It is here that "degrees" in initiation become a necessity. Every step, or passage of the candidate from a lower to a higher degree, is marked and determined finally and solely by his "proficiency in the preceding degree."

The question of Morals, or the ethical effect, therefore, is pre-determined, and as far as possible, solved first.

But even with all this wise precaution, the unprepared and the unqualified have sometimes entered the outer courts; and when compelled at last to reveal their character, have turned to rend their teachers, and have done their utmost to destroy the School and demoralize mankind.

If these moral renegades could only realize the *meaning to themselves* of thus entering the "Left-hand Path" of devolution and of starting voluntarily "down the deep descent," as portrayed in Dante's "Inferno," or in Ahrinzeman, they would, indeed, hesitate long before "turning to the left," for inevitable destruction lies that way.

Here lies the scientific explanation of the "Fall of Lucifer," portrayed in some form in the pantheons and mythologies of every philosophy and religion known to man.

The ordinary "sinner" may yet possess an "average" of all the virtues, and the ordinary "saint" an "average" of all the vices. Concerning these it was said, "I would have you either hot or cold, but because ye are neither hot nor cold, I have spewed you out of my mouth." No lukewarm soul ever entered the Kingdom of Heaven.

But a time at last comes when the soul of man, enmeshed in the "lusts of the flesh and the deceitfulness of riches," *must make his choice*. He *realizes* that he can no longer "serve two masters." He will make his choice knowingly, deliberately, and voluntarily. Happy and blessed will be he if with his whole soul, and with every impulse of his being, he declares, "I know not what others may do, *but as for me and my house, we will serve the Lord*."

If there are real Masters (and there are), they have to work under both Natural and Divine Law, and in strict harmony with the higher evolution of the whole human race.

It is only a low, feeble, and undeveloped intelligence that finds God and Nature at cross-purposes.

He who has found "the place of peace," harmonized his own nature, purified his own life, and elevated all his desires and aspirations, has discerned the "harmony of the morning stars," and caught the symphony of the heavenly hosts. In other words, he is already functioning on the Spiritual Plane.

This would seem to make clear the ethical problem raised, the stress placed upon it, and how it is met and answered by every genuine Initiate throughout the ages.

It has to be solved *first* in each individual case. Only "he who *lives the life* shall know the doctrine," or advance to power.

# CHAPTER XV

## THE SCIENCE OF PSYCHOLOGY AS A KNOWLEDGE OF THE HUMAN SOUL

The writer of the present treatise is quite well aware that the great majority of intelligent and educated people at the present day will deny that any real knowledge of the human soul as a spiritual entity, separable from the physical body during life and demonstrably surviving its death, exists now, has heretofore existed, or, if possible for man, is likely to exist for some time to come. Some will unhesitatingly declare such a thing *unknowable* for man.

I hold the firm *conviction* that this knowledge has been for ages the possession of certain individuals, few in number in any age or country, and that this knowledge has resulted through conformity to certain definite and specific requirements, formulated under well-known laws of man's spiritual being, involving a definite individual experience and resulting in a scientific and exact demonstration.

I ask the reader to note two points in the foregoing statement: First, that for myself I use the word "conviction," and not "knowledge"; and, second, that the demonstration of real knowledge referred to, is made by, and confined to an individual, in each instance.

With these individuals the knowledge is a *scientific demonstration through personal experience*. With me, the "firm conviction" is a matter of "circumstantial evidence," supported by analogy, and fortified by empirical testimony, such as acquaint the world with the facts and findings of science, and which I think admit of no other consistent and rational interpretation.

In the foregoing pages I have endeavored to give outlines, analogies, and suggestions which seem to fortify the conviction referred to.

While these are fragmentary and desultory, owing to the fact that the circumstances are so varied, the subject so vast, and the materials so abundant, yet, taken as a whole, they seem overwhelming, and, except to the careful, persistent, and intelligent student, confusing.

It must be clearly apprehended that no one familiar with the subject can reasonably suppose, nor has it ever been claimed by a real Master of the "Art," that this knowledge ever has been, or can be, communicated to, or acquired by groups of individuals at any time, or under any circumstances.

Through all the past, and at the present time, it is designated as an *individual experience*.

True, the ethics, and the philosophy, and even the principles of exact psychic science that in the past constituted the "Lesser Mysteries," can be, and often have been, taught to groups, or classes.

In the present "School of Natural Science," this preparatory training constitutes the "Ethical Section."

But above and beyond all the foregoing general considerations the "empirical facts" and the "circumstantial evidence," if we know personally one who claims to have had the specific instruction, the personal experience, and to have made the scientific demonstration referred to and outlined in the problem, our opportunity for instruction, and for the application of tests for validity and reasonableness as to the whole problem, is exceedingly valuable.

This personal acquaintance may become the nearest possible criterion, short of our own personal experience, as to demonstration.

In previous chapters this phase of the subject has, perhaps, been sufficiently dwelt upon.

The Master may say, "I know; I have had the personal experience; I have demonstrated."

The student may at last say, "I believe; I am convinced; I am satisfied."

All through the foregoing pages the effort has continually been made to preserve clearly this distinction.

In tracing analogies through the history of the past, the conditions, premonitory, present, and subsequent to great world-movements have often been referred to.

Nothing is more common or more patent than the oft-repeated saying, "This is the age of science." Any great movement that undertakes at the present day to deal with the deeper problems of individual and social life, must fit in and conform to the "spirit of the present age."

To that platform it must appeal; in that language it must be addressed, and by such judgment and criterion must it stand or fall.

All these tests and criteria have been fully met by the School of Natural Science, and they are clearly outlined and set forth in the "Great Work," addressed to "the Progressive Intelligence of the Age."

There need be no misconception or misinterpretation at this point.

It is true that superficial thinkers and readers, enthusiasts and emotionalists, are likely to infer that the science of the soul can now be had "for a consideration" and in "a dozen easy lessons."

All such are doomed to disappointment.

It is furthermore likely, if the average "physical scientist" pays any heed at all, that he will devise a series of "tests" and "experiments" of his own, to fit his preconceived notion of things psychical, with the latent conviction, at least, that he will be able to prove the whole thing a humbug.

These, also, are doomed to disappointment. Physical tests of psychical and spiritual laws and processes are unscientific. No spiritual problem can be solved in terms of physical matter alone.

So-called psychological science to-day is in the condition of one possessing a fine piece of ground, and gathering materials for a house, a superstructure.

The ground is already covered with bricks and stones, and sand and lumber, piled in every direction, with the purpose of one day beginning the work of construction, and the slogan, "Wait! Not yet!" "Some day we are hoping to build."

No architect, "no designs on the trestle-board," and so they go on accumulating "facts" and "evidence" day after day, year after year, century after century.

They have a "working hypothesis," but no definite *theorem*, and they may work till doomsday on this line without a glimmer of real scientific knowledge of the human soul, yet with mountains of "facts" or of "rubbish."

They can never prove the existence of a *spiritual entity* in terms of matter on the physical plane.

Their work has been, and still is, of great interest and value, but it is in no scientific sense, *Constructive*, backed by the laws of proportion and harmony, nor the "Canon of Architecture."

The apotheosis of Natural Science is like the "canon of proportion" in architecture, introduced by Vitruvius (an Initiate) centuries ago. It is the verification of Plato's saying, "God geometrizes," and his concept of "the World of Divine Ideas."

Plato further declares, "He who knows not the common things of life is a brute among men. He who knows the common things of life is a man among brutes. But he who knows all that can be learned by diligent inquiry is a god among men."

Natural Science, as shown in the Great Work, includes scientific knowledge on all planes of being on which the soul of man functions: The physical, moral, psychical, and spiritual; for man is a composite being.

The apotheosis of Natural Science, therefore, is Fact, Law, Demonstration, and Knowledge; before theory, conjecture, creed, dogma, superstition, or fear, intuition, inspiration, revelation, and "holy men" or "holy books" that must be accepted without evidence, or "believed" against evidence.

The *Avatars* of all the past have originated great reformations which have at last degenerated into dogma and superstition.

The people, incapable of understanding the Law, have been taught in parables, while the few in all religions and in every age have apprehended the law and learned the "Secret Doctrine."

To-day, for the first time in centuries, for the reasons already assigned, and in keeping with the scientific spirit of the age, and because superstition in power, dogma, and persecution are politically dethroned, these great truths, this Great Work, is openly declared and outlined so that he who wills may apprehend.

Let no one say, "This is an effort to *deify* an individual." It *is* an effort to enthrone Truth; to remove the barriers to the rights of conscience, the shackles of reason, private judgment and Individual Responsibility, and to free the soul of man from all the fetters of ignorance, superstition, and fear, in order that he may be "first a man," "then a Master," and at length on a higher plane of being, something more than man has yet realized, or ever dreamed.

Something "that eye hath not seen, nor ear heard, nor hath it yet entered into the heart of man to conceive the glory that shall be revealed."

The beginning is here and now, when man shall achieve the Mastery of Self and really possess his own soul, and not hold it tremblingly as a *pawn* of some pretentious potentate of the soul.

The right of Light, Knowledge, and further progress by *"Being a Man,"* and not a chattel, an asset, a pawn, or a slave.

This is the coming *Avatar*, and the dawn is already here.

Will the day darken, the Light be quenched? Who can tell?

The redemption of Woman from the slavery of all the past is well under way, and it is indeed a glorious sign.

No lesson in history is plainer nor more readily demonstrated than the fact that the degeneracy of a religion and the degradation of woman go hand in hand.

Demonstrate to-day in any country on earth the status of woman as a whole, and no mistake need be made as to the prevailing religion.

Woman's political disability is another matter  entirely; for she is dominated by man only because, and only so far as, she is handicapped or degraded by the dominant religion.

Take woman from the churches, Protestant or Romish, to-day, and no church could do business for a twelvemonth.

For these reasons the immense and rapidly growing movements, Women's Clubs and the like, to-day, are of great significance, backed and illuminated as they are by all past history.

In the new movement, the School of Natural Science, the door is as wide open to woman as to man. I might paraphrase the slogan of the Robber Barons of the middle ages. *"She* may seize who hath the power, *She* may hold who can."

In the coming Illuminati woman will stand by the side of man in all opportunity, endeavor, or achievement.

In the new age woman will be something few men have even yet dreamed of.

We might call this new age "*the Woman's Avatar*," without doing violence to either religion, tradition, history, or science; while the sacred Hymns of the Vedas, with the angel of the household and the inspirer of the soul of man, the worship of Divinity, by both men and women, opened a new heaven on this old earth.

And then—such children as will be born, without pain, not through chance, caprice, nor under protest, but even as they were in Greece, as an  offering of Love on the altar of divine man-womanhood, with a song of joy to heaven.

Prof. Fiske somewhere said, "The evolution of man by Natural Selection draws near its close, to be followed by that of Divine Selection."

The Divinity *in* man is *Christos*, the "son of the Father," the Divine and Eternal *Avatar*.

Belief is rather a superficial process, the intellect ("mortal mind") mingled with the emotions, changing and evanescent. "Now you see it, and now you don't." It is mingled with hope that alternates with fear and doubt.

Faith, when once analyzed and apprehended, is another thing entirely, though nearly every one, and most writers, confuse "belief" and "faith."

"Faith is the soul's *intuitive conviction* of that which both *Reason* and *Conscience* approve."

Genuine faith rarely wavers or changes, because it is an evolution, a "growth of the soul," a spiritual experience, and it becomes the "dominant chord" in the symphony of life, determining Harmony.

It is in this deliberate and discriminative sense that I have used the term *conviction* in relation to the Master and his "Great Work." He never dogmatizes, nor undertakes to "indoctrinate."

In answer to a question on some deep and perplexing problem of the soul or of the spiritual plane, he replies, "So far as we *know*, it is so and so." "A new experience, or an added light, may alter our conclusion."

The average individual scarcely realizes what absolute sincerity, with no motive save Love of Truth, and beneficence to man guided by clear intelligence, and dominated by the rational Will, means, or can accomplish.

These are the natural powers of the human soul. There is nothing mysterious or miraculous about them, more than in the art of music of a Beethoven or a Paganini, or in gymnastics and the winner of the Marathon.

"To *shape* and *use*, arise and fly,
The reeling Faun, the sensual feast,
Move upward, working out the beast,
And let the ape and tiger die."

My *conviction* is strong, and my Faith unwavering.

"The great and peaceful ones live, regenerating the world like the coming of spring: and having themselves crossed the ocean of embodied existence, help those who try to do the same thing without personal motive." ("Crest Jewel of Wisdom.")

# CHAPTER XVI

## THE NEW AVATAR

From all the foregoing general considerations it may be discerned that the "New Avatar" is strictly that of *Scientific Demonstration*.

As we use terms in vogue at the present day, it pertains to the field of Natural Science.

This does not imply that it is irreligious, nor unreligious, nor sacrilegious.

When it is clearly apprehended it will be found to be the only thing that harmonizes—not the Institutions of man— but Science, Philosophy, and Religion *per se*, as departments in human intelligence.

Man will thus discern "the rational order that pervades the universe."

The purpose and result of such knowledge to man are Harmony, Enlightenment, Courage, and Hope.

Man *is* the arbiter of his own destiny. He may *become* the Master of his own Fate. Such are the *Illuminati*, the "Masters of the Great White Lodge," the Benefactors of the whole human race, the members of the "School of Natural Science."

What would I have my readers do? I answer, *Investigate*! Study! Think! Wait! Hope! Anticipate!

Careful, intelligent, and conscientious investigation will determine the fact that we possess in America to-day *one* who can fill all the requirements that I have endeavored to designate and portray—not as a "reincarnation" of Buddha or Jesus, but as a "Master"—one who has been duly instructed and prepared, who has had the personal experience, and has made a *practical demonstration*, that determines Mastership.

He has demonstrated that "there is no death," but transition only (except through conscious and determined devolution, or *suicide of the soul*). Man is, after all, and in the last analysis, a "free moral agent."

As a Member of the "Great School" he was educated and initiated many years ago, and has consecrated his life to this service. He has demonstrated the separability of the soul by leaving and returning to his body at will.

The School of Natural Science; the Great Work; the Individual Representative; the conditions of the present age; the opportunities offered; the demand for real knowledge everywhere; the falling in pieces of creeds and dogmas; the expectancy so often voiced—all of these correspond intimately with what the ancient Aryans designated as "*Avataric.*"

It is not now the deification of any Individual, but the "*apotheosis of Natural Science*," as the foundation and method in the achievement of actual knowledge.

From this actual knowledge will arise a new Faith, not a new religion, but the old Religion of Humanity, precisely as taught and lived by Jesus, Christna, Buddha, and all the other "Redeemers," and real Avatars of the past.

The "Enemy of all Righteousness," as already said, have made many attempts to assassinate this Representative of the Great School, but he goes steadily about his own work. These enemies realize the danger to their unholy work, but not the *Power* back of this great movement. This they can never destroy.

The day of enlightenment has come, and the cry has gone forth, Ho! all ye who are heavy-laden, involved in fear and doubt and uncertainty; bewildered, discouraged, despairing, and committing suicide! There is no death! Man is the Arbiter of his own Fate! Look up and Live, and Hope and *Realize*!

And there shall dawn for you a new heaven and a new earth in which dwelleth Love and Peace and Righteousness; with Jesus—the *Christos*—your "elder Brother," leading the way, and the downtrodden, the poor and despised children of men, shouting Hosanna! for the Loving Kindness that will have taken the place of selfishness, strife, cruelty, superstition, and Dogma.

Religion will no longer be a matter of mere sentiment, nor of emotion, of blind belief, nor of fear, superstition, dogma, nor creed—but a *Great Work*. So Mote it be.

The author of this volume can lay no claim for it as a systematic treatise on Psychology, either according to the rules of composition or the orderly sequence of science.

It is rather a number of essays, some of which were written without reference to publication, or the design, at the time, of putting them together in a single volume.

There is, therefore, more or less repetition, the same subject under a different title, viewed from a different aspect, yet involving the same principles, motives, and aims.

But the subject of Psychology is so vast, so intricate, so interesting and important, and yet, in the average mind, so confused, and so little known, that considerations from many sides, and even repetitions in the application of a given principle in various ways, are believed more likely to make the whole subject apprehensible to the general reader to whom it is addressed.

Moreover, the author believes that the time has come when Psychology, as a *Constructive Science* of the nature, laws, and destiny of the Human Soul, need no longer be regarded as unknown or unattainable, but open to all who seek it in the right way, giving to it the consideration, time, and loyalty it so amply deserves.

To such as these, it is hoped, the foregoing pages  may give many clews and sidelights, suggestions, encouragement, and hope.

Psychology, to the Author of this volume, means literally *A Knowledge of the Human Soul*, rather than of treatises upon the subject, or of the opinions, beliefs, or dogmas of men.

www.ingramcontent.com/pod-product-compliance
Lightning Source LLC
Chambersburg PA
CBHW070642290526
45790CB00001B/165